THE
ANIMALS' PARABLE

BY KEITH KORMAN

A LIBERTY ISLAND BOOK
ISBN: 978-1-947942-00-4

Eden
The Animal's Parable
© 2017 by Keith Korman
Illustrations by Lisa Paris
All Rights Reserved

This book is a work of fiction. People, places, events, and situations are the product of the author's imagination. Any resemblance to actual persons, living or dead, or historical events, is purely coincidental.

No part of this book may be reproduced, stored in a retrieval system, or transmitted by any means without the written permission of the author and publisher.

LIBERTY ISLAND
LET YOUR INNER ROBIN HOOD FREE

Liberty Island
libertyislandmag.com

Published in the United States of America

Table of Contents

The Legion 1
Three Kings 10
Flight into Egypt 17
Nazareth 25
The Essene 32
The River 36
The Wilderness 46
A Wedding 56
Judas 63
Signs and Wonders 71
Wind and Waves 83
The Women 89
Come Forth 103
Palm Fronds 114
By What Authority 119
I Know Where He Will Be 125
Bread and Wine 131
The Garden 136
Denial 146
Let the Romans Decide 151
INRI 170
Two Nights and a Day 184

If you have a soul—that's where the wild trespass.

Also the Angels.
—Theron Raines 1925–2012

For the lads, Ari and Vali—heirs to the Riddle of the Stones

Before

There is not enough darkness in the world to extinguish a single candle flame.
—*Saint Francis of Assisi*

The Legion
✳ ✳ ✳

The Roman Legionaries called the dog Old Gray. During the day his ashen fur made him look like a wolf, while at night the moon turned his coat silver from head to tail. Season after season Old Gray kept pace with the soldiers' column, trotting beside their tramping feet. No one knew where he had come from, but as long as anyone could recall the dog had marched with the cohort, camp to camp. Out of companionship? Or for the scraps of Roman bread and soup at day's end?

Maybe both.

When winter came and the weather grew cold Old Gray took shelter in their tents. In the heat of summer he lay on a folded cloak under the starry sky. Like all dogs he slept lightly, his ears and nose alert to any strange movement near at hand. And so Old Gray earned his keep, guarding the soldiers of the Legion.

That winter the Roman army marched south many miles through endless barren hills and Old Gray kept pace, trotting mile after mile. Oftentimes he scouted ahead, then doubled back, only to overhear the cavalry horses who grumbled at every turn of the road.

For weeks on end the warhorses whinnied the same complaint:

"No grass. No grass."

Then grimly to anyone within earshot:

"Bare ground. Everywhere bare ground."

The column's surly mule, harnessed to the hay wagon laden with the Legions' grub and the animals' daily feed, grumbled along with the rest, "I have grass. Bales and bales of grass. They'll feed you tonight, like they do every night. Be thankful you don't have to pull it."

It was a soldier's right to gripe. Mules and horses no exception. Old Gray took it in stride. Mules and horses could only graze if there was grass, while smart old dogs combed the roadside for birds' eggs and every creature of the field. But Old Gray didn't feel too sorry for the mules or horses; the soldiers always fed the beasts of burden first as the cohort wouldn't move without the draft animals lugging food and water and the officers never traveled on foot.

Every day, the barren road into the south stretched to oblivion. The column plodding on forever, a great serpent of men fading into the cloud of yellow dust that hovered over their line of march. The hills of this wilderness were mostly barren, but then they came upon flocks. Old Gray saw shepherds, their sheep straying for tufts and brambles in the rocky pastures above the road. At dusk Old Gray crept up the slope and found what he was looking for—a ewe and her lamb astray.

At first the shepherd tried to strike the thieving dog with his crook, crying, "Get away! Get away!" But Old Gray darted off, herding the ewe and her lamb down the slope as the man stumbled in pursuit. Back in camp Old Gray was praised by all who saw him and the clink of Roman coins quieted the shepherd's protest. Anything to shut him up.

Old Gray had heard it all before.

The herdsman retreated back up the pasture still griping about his poor lambs and stingy Roman soldiers. But at least he'd been paid.

The next day the column marched on, their endless tramp indistinguishable from the day before. The dog hated this place; a land of bitter smoke, of dust, of stamping feet, too harsh for man or beast.

"What's your name?" Old Gray asked the ewe.

"They call me Honey," the sheep panted. "Because the bees follow me through the flowers in the spring. You see, they follow me yet." Just as she said, two large, fat bees lazily circled her head. She fell in with some of the other cattle, several cows, a few pigs and goats marching beside the soldiers, until Old Gray told the ewe and her lamb, "I found you, you're mine. You march with us."

The rest of the day, Honey said little else. And after the first mile the bees vanished, buzzing back whence they came.

But sheep were used to grazing, not marching. Soon the dust rimed the ewe's nostrils, and her hooves hurt. Worried, Honey bleated for her lamb to stay abreast; and it was all the little one could do to keep up. At the end of the first day's march the ewe had stopped giving milk and Honey had lost track of her child. The road was killing them both.

That night the ewe stood some distance off, not wanting to be near the soldiers' camp fire, not wanting to be with Old Gray. They tied her to a heavy shield, but Honey made no effort to escape. And so the fire burned, meat was shared and the night passed to the sound of snoring men.

The next day's march her lamb was nowhere to be seen, and the ewe barely kept pace with the column, so Old Gray hurried her along, nipping at her rear legs whenever she slowed.

"Last night you sat by the fire while the soldiers turned the spit," she cried. "How dare you snap at me now?"

Old Gray thought for a moment.

"It takes more than bees and flowers to walk the earth," he growled.

Then after a breath, "You're either watching the spit or on it."

That day's march Honey lagged farther and farther behind, as if she knew what awaited her.

Old Gray knew.

Soon there'd be another sheep for the coals.

At length the Legionaries reached the walls of a stone city, the dog following the soldiers down narrow streets into the heart of the citadel. After twists and turns the column halted before the high temple. The great wooden doors stood open to the Romans, but within the doorway hung long linen panels. A cloth wall draped from the lintel, dividing the common street from the sanctuary. Embroidered in scarlet and purple and blue, great radiant veils showed the heavens and earth as made by Him those first six days.

Without waiting for an invitation, the Roman horses brushed aside the dazzling curtains and passed into the courtyard. Old Gray came in with the first of the horsemen and no one dared to stop the dog.

For a moment he paused to stare at these long lengths of cloth. He could smell the scents of a thousand animals within their weave: goats and birds and bulls. He could smell a thousand humans within the fabric: merchants from across the great sea, the harsh sweat of slaves and supplicants, even the faint scent of priests—dry, old pious men. These hanging curtains still held the touch of everything that passed between them. Wise, bright curtains, protecting the courtyard of the temple grounds, witness to all who entered. Good men and bad.

As the dog followed the soldiers, the priests in their robes fell to bended knee. Old Gray passed row after row of prostrate figures—as if by offering their necks to a dog and the mighty Legionaries the old men might save their heads. The horsemen climbed the many steps and the priests shuffled aside, cowering as the animals strode into the sanctum.

But Old Gray did not follow the horses. Instead he lingered by the stone altar. And once again he found a lamb, this one tied to an iron ring. The lamb reminded him of Honey but this one's fleece was finer than that of any sheep of the hills. The sacrificial lamb looked at Old Gray with liquid eyes as if to plead for help.

"How did you come here?" Old Gray asked.

The lamb shook her chain. "This morning I was outside the city walls but my master led me in. Many hands took me and now I am here. They say he sold me for my beautiful fleece. But I'm not sure that's true." The chain clanked. She tugged on her collar; her fleece rubbed away, neck raw. "Now my coat is ruined."

The Roman dog looked at the lamb with pity, but said nothing. You either wore a collar or you didn't. Old Gray's own neck had grown so used to the studded leather he barely noticed its grip. Just then the cavalry rode out the sanctum doors, stepping over the bodies of the prostrate priests. The Roman horses swept across the compound, tramped over every flagstone and left dung in every corner of the temple.

The lamb's eyes pleaded with Old Gray, begging him to free her, to lead her away. The dog met the lamb's gaze.

"You'll be coming with us," the dog told her.

"Are you taking me somewhere nice?" the lamb asked.

Old Gray thought of Honey, fallen by the wayside as one of the soldiers unfastened the lamb's collar.

"That's never up to me," the dog said. "At least you'll be off that ring."

Old Gray and the lamb followed the cavalry from the temple compound and trotted side by side through the paved streets. Neither spoke. The city stones burned in the sun, while the doors and alleys on every side stumbled past like gaps in a labyrinth. The noon heat struck in full as they reached their final destination. The garrison.

The great cedar door groaned open and the Roman Legionaries wearily filed in. A sentry clanged spear to shield as the commander rode under the arch. The Legionary who had freed the lamb dragged her inside by a rope. She glanced once at Old Gray standing in the street, her terrified eyes pleading, *help*! But Old Gray did nothing.

You either turned the spit or—

The two watchdogs that guarded the garrison charged out the gateway, leapt across the threshold and lunged into the street—only to be yanked back on their chains. Their paws scrabbled on the stone steps. Teeth bared, lips snarling, "No camp followers here, not here, not here! Get lost! Scram!"

They kept barking, until the sentry clanged his spear to shield again and shouted, "Shut up, both of you! Shut up!"

The metal door ground closed. The guard dogs' growls faded from inside and the garrison walls stared down at Old Gray in the street. The sentry leaned his spear and shield against the stone and sat on a wooden stool. He uncorked a water bottle and took a swig. After recorking the bottle the man closed his eyes, leaned back against the hot stones and quietly began to snore.

Old Gray didn't know what to do. So he sat in the street by a merchant's stall to think matters through. Even under the awnings' shade, the sun beat the ground and the streets smelled of human stink. Old Gray sniffed at the canvas of a butcher's stand with its hanging meat; the surly merchant threw a handful of pebbles and cursed, "Lousy dog. Get lost."

No one offered Old Gray water.

No one offered him food.

No one offered him a place to lie down.

This city was no place for him. And the Legion would always choose mutton over a marching dog. The garrison doors shut tight against camp followers.

Before sunset the Romans' watchdog no longer belonged to the Legion. Old Gray found another caravan of camels and mules heading from the city. And as he once came south, now he traveled north. The camels looked down their noses refusing to speak, but the poky mules let him walk in their shadow. One in particular sighed as he trotted along beside her. She'd been on this route before, complaining at the packs of bound wool on her truss, "Oh so heavy, so heavy. So many miles, so many."

Old Gray knew this kind of work—march along during the day, sleep at night beside a fire. Wake the travelers at the first sign of trouble. But this caravan wasn't like the Romans' column; they didn't scavenge the countryside, and only ate what they brought with them. Food was scarce, and Old Gray rummaged the fire pits for burnt bones in the morning. After two days' march he was weary, hungry and parched. He'd lapped some muddy puddles, but no one gave him so much as a crust. And his fellow animals were no help at all.

The camels couldn't care less: "We carry our water with us. Get a hump so you can drink." And the donkey no better:

"Perhaps if you wear a truss to carry wool they'll give you water." Hard to think such creatures were worse than soldiers. At least soldiers knew a dog's worth when they needed one.

Tongue hanging out, Old Gray stopped in his tracks.

There was something familiar about this stretch of hills, the scent of sweetness in the air, orange blossom, yes, *there*—bees flitting from flower to flower up the rocky slope. And boxes where the bees gathered, yes, *honey*. Deep in the pasture a fat ewe suckled a baby lamb. The mother lamb looked down at him with peaceful eyes, her infant at her teat. All was right with the world. And Old Gray knew where he was.

The shepherd's dog met him halfway up the slope. And Old Gray could see the mutt was even older than himself. Creaky on his legs and near toothless.

"Who goes there?" the Ancient growled. "Friend or foe?"

"I've been here before," Old Gray told the Ancient.

"You!" The Ancient immediately knew the stranger. "You were the one who took poor Honey," he growled. "*For shame.* You took her while I slept."

Old Gray bowed his head. "I did. That was my job."

But what was done was done; he met the Ancient's eyes and circled cautiously.

What now?

"I saw the bees," Old Gray told him. "I'm done with marching." He was close to exhaustion, and nearly wild with thirst. "Is there no place for me here?"

The Ancient looked Old Gray nose to nose; the two dogs were almost on equal footing, and a fight now might wound or kill them both. What then of the shepherd with no one to wake him or watch for danger's approach?

"Harrumph," the Ancient grumbled, giving in. "If you know how to steal, maybe you can learn how to keep."

"I kept the Legion," Old Gray panted. "Right up till the garrison. Until they didn't need me. Now I keep it no more. Is keeping sheep more difficult?"

"Hah!" the Ancient laughed. "Only when a Legion camps nearby."

The Ancient wearily wagged his tail and shrugged. "Come along then. There's water and a fire, and maybe something left to eat. Besides there are mice out at night in the fields, if you're very desperate. And very quick."

So the two animals postponed their test of who would rule, and put their fate aside. Old Gray followed the Ancient to water in a clay bowl. That deep drink of water, the best he ever drank. There was fire and a bone. At last Old Gray closed his eyes, sinking into the lap of sleep. As the moon rose, the Legionaries' dog dreamt of poor Honey, with bees over her head and flower blossoms in her fleece. When dawn broke, the wind sighed across the pasture, a whisper of emptiness. The sheep stared silently, not one of them bending his head to graze.

"What?" Old Gray asked them. "What is it?" Then he saw the answer.

The wizened dog had gone in his sleep.

Old Gray nosed the dry, cracked muzzle, but there was no one left inside.

Time and fate had decided who would guard the flock, who would rule the pasture.

And Old Gray took the Ancient's place.

Three Kings
✷ ✷ ✷

Some years and many lambs later, the sheep of the pasture still wandered the stony slopes and Old Gray's descendants still watched over their flocks by night.

The shepherds of the hills called Old Gray's great-grandson Noah—because he protected the flocks with relentless zeal. Herding them, moving them—guarding them with open eyes while they grazed or slept. Nothing escaped his notice; not a single lamb allowed to stray, nor a single old goat allowed to wander off.

Noah sniffed every scent, inspected every blade of grass, cocking his ears forward and then laying them back behind a furrowed, pensive brow. Always alert, even to the most harmless things: snuffing at the shape of a rock in the pasture, at the scents of the flowers over the hill—cocking his head at the buzz of bees in their honeycomb crates, at the little lamb bleating for its ewe. Staring up at the stars at night, Noah watched their passage across the great arc of heaven; a dog searching for any change in the wind.

Not far off in a cleft of hills stood a little town. Noah often accompanied his herdsman there, when the man went to sell his wool or sought food or drink or company. Naturally Noah noticed there had been much traffic down on the road of late.

Events in the great wide world had stirred people from their homes. Day and night they marched along the road, in caravans or groups of two or three, or even singly. For weeks, throngs on their way from one place to another passed through the little town never to be seen again.

But why they traveled and where they were going, Noah did not know.

While hanging in the sky at night, one star seemed to travel above the endless stream of camel trains on the road, every night a little closer. Noah had watched the star move westward inch by inch all year, always brighter than the rest—until it hung nearly overhead. This night it seemed to pause motionless over the town.

For once the road below lay empty of men and mules except for one caravan, plodding wearily on. Not a very big caravan, only three camels, but the light of the star seemed to shine around them—a soft glow that enveloped the camels and their riders as they trudged along, a halo in the darkness. *What could this mean?*

Who were these travelers?

Why had they come?

Listening hard, Noah heard the mice in the fields chattering away, "See! See! Look! See!" squeaking in their high little voices mouse to mouse all the way down to the road. Each and every one of them seemed to know something special about the caravan, as if they'd heard it on the wind. And suddenly Noah knew he must see for himself.

He padded quietly down the slope, leaving the sheep sleeping in their fields.

Oddly there was no dog in the caravan, but Noah still followed at a polite distance.

After a few paces he trotted to the front.

"What is your name?" Noah asked the lead camel. "Where do you come from?" And for a moment the lead camel, like camels everywhere, merely looked down his long nose. "My name is Sharif. I am the Lead Camel. And why should we tell you?"

The dog didn't know what to say. Noah padded on in silence until the camel, perhaps taking pity on the poor dog's ignorance, deigned to answer:

"I come from Babylon. A great city to the East."

"Where else have you been?" Noah asked. This camel's hooves must have walked a mighty distance. What had he seen? Where had he been?

"Everywhere," the camel said. "And now we're here in this godforsaken back alley of the Levant." They had reached the little town. Sharif sniffed as he looked down the dusty street. Other caravans had already arrived, and camels stood or crouched uncomfortably everywhere. Merchants laid their bundles against any free wall, while other men sprawled about the paving stones, sleeping upon their goods so that none could steal them. Was there nowhere else to go?

Street after street, conditions were no better. The caravan stopped at the door of a stable. The three camels sighed with relief as their riders dismounted, and Noah shuffled out of the way. But there was no more room inside than outside. This was not a very large stable either, four stalls in all, but every stall filled. A large black donkey in one corner looked sympathetically at the newcomers.

"Oh you poor dears. My name is Mabel, but I do not think we can fit you in my stall."

No, there was barely room for the camels' noses poking in the stable door.

A cow and her calf shared another stall, wedged in tight; Mama Cow shook her head, "And don't come begging here either."

Lady Duck and her quacklings fluttered their wings in a pile of straw—while Lord Duck sat uncomfortably on a beam extremely annoyed, a scowl on his beak:

"No room!" called out Lord Duck. "No room!"

Sharif, the Lead Camel snorted. As though anyone would want to stay in their stuffy barn. "Do not fear, oh Quack, we shall not climb onto that beam with you."

But Noah couldn't care less about snooty camels or silly quackers. The star hanging in the sky stared in the stable's narrow window. Its light fell on another animal, a She-Dog lying in a corner of the stall, nursing three suckling pups. Before Noah set a single paw inside the stall the She-Dog raised a lip to him, "No closer, Nosey. Stay where you are."

"I will, I promise," Noah told her. He snuffed the straw-strewn floor for any scent of a mate. No, nothing. No rival here. She-Dog left off nuzzling her little ones and looked heavily into the darkest corner. Moments passed as the star's light crawled across the barn floor. Still others had sought shelter in the stable. Noah breathed their scents: human woman, human pup. A woman and child huddled in a mound of straw. The star in the window touched the woman's face. Like She-Dog, the woman suckled her baby.

The three caravan travelers bowed their heads and entered. Noah noticed the camel riders were old men, clad in worn and dusty robes as if they had ridden far just like Sharif had said. The three elders crept further into the stable and knelt. Yet another man came in from the shadow, lit a lantern and hung it on a beam.

The lantern cast a pale light over the wooden stalls and the cow raised her head. "Is it time to milk?" the cow asked mildly confused. Her calf looked up in silent alarm, but when no one came with a milking stool she laid her head down and snuggled back into the thick straw. "There, there now," the cow murmured to her calf as she fell back to sleep. "Nothing to worry about …"

The man with the lantern stared at the newcomers.

"These old men mean no harm," the woman told her husband. "If only we had something to offer them after their long ride."

"We left Babylon with gold and incense and myrrh," the eldest of the elders said. "But all these we lost on the road."

He held out his hand, "This only remains." In his palm sat a wafer-thin coin. It might have been shiny once upon a time, but years of passing from hand to hand had rubbed it smooth and dark, the features of the face on the coin worn away by a thousand thumbs. For a second the coin caught the lantern's light and it glittered. Gold.

The next elder offered a scrap of cloth; carefully he unfolded the threadbare rag, showing only some meager crumbs. A few morsels of incense, no more than a few moments' worth of smoke, but its scent filled the stalls with wholesomeness and peace.

The last elder took from around his neck a string to which was tied a tiny glass vial no larger than his pinky and stoppered with a tiny plug of cork. The vial looked almost empty, but at the bottom were a few drops of oil, the dregs of myrrh, barely enough medicine to heal a bee sting.

Noah knew the look and scent of all these things. The shepherds used myrrh on their cuts and scrapes. When sheep were shorn and the fleece sold, they burned incense in their huts. And every animal knew men used coins to trade for food, to buy other animals and other men.

"Now we have nothing but what we wear," the eldest of the elders said. "Still, it is for us to offer, not you to give. And all we offer is our company. We need no lantern to show us what we seek."

"Then sit and rest the night with us," the man said. "All are welcome here."

Lord Duck ruffled his wings on the beam. "Will you put out that light! Can't you see some of us are trying to sleep?" Gently, the man put his lips to the lantern door and blew the flame away. From the open window the starlight returned, leaving the woman's face and child at her breast glowing faintly.

Outside the sound of coarse laughter came from a nearby crowded inn. Revelers too full of wine stumbled down the street singing a muddled song, then turned down an alley and the rough voices faded. But the dog caught the scent of food on the men, and Noah knew what to do. Around the side of the inn by the fire tables, the cook was throwing out yesterday's bread and soft melons and bits of gristle. Food for rats. Noah knew it was now or never. In a very few moments squealers would descend from every corner to fight over every scrap.

The bits of meat were good, the bits of bread too. Noah cautiously brought a heel of bread to She-Dog, and paused. Her eyes glinted with hunger. He carefully laid the bread by her paws, but out of snapping distance. She snuffed at it, then in a flash leaned forward and snatched the bread in her teeth. She swallowed and licked her lips. Her eyes had changed; now gleaming as if to say, *All right, you can stay in the corner under the Duck. Just don't come near the pups.*

What do I call her? Noah wondered. And She-Dog seemed to read his mind.

"Call me ... Sheba."

Noah made five trips, five trips for the gristle and stale crusts. Five times she looked at him with the same hard eyes, but by and by Sheba's gaze softened. Her whelps slept. Then she too laid down her head.

Above the town the lonely strain of a ram's horn rose into the hills.

First one horn called out and then another rang in answer—the call of heralds telling of the star, telling of the stable, and blessing all who sheltered there. For word had passed in the night, a whisper of hope in the midst of the darkness. Horns of praise and awe, for word had come even to the shepherds of the hills as they crouched among their flocks. Words drifting upon the night wind and silken sky—that as of now, this moment, today and forever—all would be forgiven, all would be redeemed.

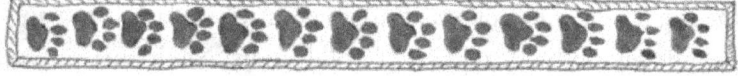

Flight into Egypt
✳ ✳ ✳

Night passed slowly. Noah watched the star set and a sliver of moon take its place, shedding a colder light. The elders slept fitfully in the straw, close enough to Lady Duck and her quacklings for Lord Duck to complain, "Stop snoring." But soon he ruffled his feathers, gave up for the night and tucked his beak under a wing.

Noah could not sleep. After all, he mostly kept watch at night on the hilly pasture and slept during the day when the shepherds were awake. But something else troubled him; the light from the moon cast a dark shadow in his mind. Quietly, so as not to disturb Sheba, her pups, the sleeping family or even the snoring old men … he padded to the barn door and went outside. The camels drowsed heavily on their bony knees, nodding their heads, not bothering to look up at his passing. All around him the sounds of the town were muted in the dead of night. Even the cats and the rats seemed to be hiding in silence. A quiet voice called Noah's eyes to the horizon, the faintest whisper to his ears—and there up on the stony ridge the dog saw the horsemen.

Noah smelled the scent of leather and sweat, and then heard the faint rattle of armor, spear and sword, the clinks of saddle and harness. Horsemen like those his great-grandsire, Old Gray, had marched alongside into the stone city …

And in a flash Noah knew the horsemen had come to kill. You could always tell—the horses gave off the lather of fear. Did the horses themselves even know what was to come with blinders on? Noah knew like a picture in his mind: the charge of hooves, the singing of spears and great lamentation, women begging for mercy and the moans of despair fleeing down every alley in the little town.

Now the dog's only thought was to get the barn awake. But even as he snuffed at one sleeper and another, they grumbled at him. Noah nudged the elders, nudged and prodded. But instead of rising, the eldest of the elders mumbled an oath and pushed him away and rolled over. He snuffled Yosef, the husband. The man mumbled as if in a dream, but didn't wake. And he tried Maryam, the mother, but she too slept deeply with the child in her arms.

Sheba looked at him with skeptical eyes. "What is it now?"

"Horses and men! Horsemen on the ridge!" he growled at her. "We have to leave, we have to get away. *Get away now.*"

Lord Duck scolded Noah from his perch on the beam, "Didn't I tell you there's no room up here! Go back to sleep!"

Scared and frustrated Noah rushed outside once more, almost frantic. The horsemen hadn't moved from the ridge, but he knew, *he knew* they'd move soon. Then in a flash—the camels! The camels might help him, if they weren't too superior to understand. Noah snapped and yapped, first at their knees and then at their rumps, "Wake up!"

Sharif the Lead Camel snorted, "Stop woofing, will you? There's nothing to see, nothing to do!"

"Get up!" Noah barked, "Get up or I'll bite your tail!"

Eden

Slowly the camels unfolded themselves, groaning with displeasure at this annoying dog.

"Have you no manners? I hope my rider beats you," one Camel groaned.

"You have no authority here!" the second Camel wheezed. "Who made you master?"

While Sharif the Lead Camel grunted, "I spit at you. *Ptui!* Go away!"

But by this time Sheba had risen from her pups and joined him. One look at the ridge, and she understood.

"You are right, we must go. But what shall I do with my pups? There are too many to carry!"

"We shall carry them no matter what," Noah told her. "None shall be left behind."

Even now Yosef the husband came to the barn door, while the elders stumbled close behind. They stared upon the stony ridge under the cold light of the moon. "Just like in my dream," the husband murmured in fear.

"Herod!"

And suddenly in the gasp of that one name they understood.

"We have no time to lose," Yosef said to Maryam. In three shakes of a lamb's tail the donkey was bridled, the camels saddled and the child gathered to his mother's breast to ride. Yosef hoisted their goods onto his shoulders: his tools, their bedrolls, the cooking gear, but there was too much for a man to carry so he slung the extra across Mabel, their beast of burden.

Mabel the donkey shook her head at Mama Cow in dismay. "Mama Cow, I am so tired. You are so lucky to stay here and never carry a load."

But Mama Cow was no luckier than the rest. The cow and the calf were rounded up with everyone else—everyone but

Sheba's pups. The She-Dog looked at her poor whelps mewling on the straw. No provision had been made for them, and Sheba circled the three pups frantically, round and round: which one to take first, which one to leave?

Lord Duck, Lady Duck and their quacklings tut-tutted from their wicker basket hanging on the side of the donkey. "No room!"

Noah tugged the sleeve of Yosef's robe.

He didn't understand. "What now?"

"Do something! Do something!" Sheba cried.

No, this would not do. Noah barred the door, planted his feet and bared his teeth, if the pups didn't leave, nobody left—*Now do you understand?*

The husband picked up a stick, but his gentle wife stayed his hand. "Bring the pups," Maryam told him. "Bring the pups and they'll follow. Bring the pups and no harm will come to us. We'll feed her and she'll feed them. And we'll need a bold dog too."

And finally Yosef understood his wife. The woman was right.

So they brought everyone and everything, first loading the old men on their camels, clapping wicker covers over the silly ducks in baskets to keep them in line, then prodding Mabel the donkey to get her going. They tied Sheba's three pups in a shawl on Maryam's back, and tugged the balky cow and her calf by a rope, now more confused than ever.

"Are we going somewhere?" Mama Cow asked. "A better place to milk?"

But no one replied; too hurried to answer.

They left by the low road, avoiding the ridge, and vanished into the desert on a whisper of wind.

Dawn found them miles from the little town, and even as the sun climbed into the sky they heard the echo of a cry behind them. Not just children's cries, but crying young ones of every kind—moppets and pups, kittens and little angels, even ducklings and chicks, all fell under the hooves of the horsemen and their spears. The cries rose behind them like a cloud. Indeed, a cloud of red dust rose from the little town, a spreading stain, befouling the sky for all to see.

"Don't look," Sharif the Lead Camel said. Then the cow to her calf, "Keep up now." And Mabel the donkey, "These burdens do not feel so heavy after all." And finally Lord Duck with a peaked wan look on his bill, "Plenty of room now. But let's *not* go back."

Noah and Sheba picked up the pace, even as the sands of the wilderness passed under their paws.

After many leagues the wayfarers camped by the long river amongst the nameless huts of reeds, where the river people caught fish in nets and hunted the bank for waterfowl and their eggs. For some weeks the elders too, rested in the bosom of their new family. Yosef set about to make a low table. He then unloaded his tools upon it and offered to work on the caravans as they halted by the ferryman. For many wagons and bands of travelers came out of the wilderness, hurrying from troubles behind and hoping for the best.

Sheba lay fat and happy by the water's edge. She nursed her pups, occasionally snapping at flies but eating her fill every day of fish and the rabbits Noah caught in the sandy dunes beside the waters.

In time the three camels and their elders departed, not

content to stay by the bulrushes that grew on the great river's bank. They went to seek what lay beneath the star as it moved across the heavens, whether its light shone into the hearts of men in distant lands ... or left no mark. Each of the wise men carried one of Sheba's pups with them for remembrance and love, promising wherever they wandered, whatever path they took, no harm would come to Sheba's offspring. And each wise man vowed to return in the fullness of time, but none was ever seen again in the land of the great king's horsemen.

Noah and Sheba stayed by the river and guarded the family. Over time She-Dog bore Noah more pups and they too kept watch. At last rumors came to the riverbank that in the stone city the King of the Horsemen was no more.

A wandering shepherd sold Yosef two ewes and a lamb. He also bore news of great events. At last more than rumors came to the riverbank. The shepherd told them the people of the countryside no longer feared soldiers at their doors and now it would be safe to return. The great King of the Horsemen was truly dead.

Mabel the donkey complained as always, the ducks made fools of themselves in their baskets and the little herd of two ewes and a lamb followed obediently behind, however many miles they traveled. Alas, the road back was no longer empty as during their flight. Countless crosses studded the roadside bearing the hanging remains of those who had displeased the late great king.

Noah and Sheba often paused under the shadows of the timber to smell what had happened there—but the knowledge always came to the same cruel end. A man had died and given the flies a home.

"There is nothing for us here," Noah told Sheba. And the

two dogs could not bear to see their famished brethren feasting on the dead. They hurried on, afraid to tarry.

Before long the travelers passed the town of the stable with the stalls. There was plenty of room now in the barn, but they pushed on. The town of the star had forgotten them.

Indeed all the world had forgotten them, and at last they returned to their own village in the north and found an abandoned dwelling where a carpenter could measure, saw and hammer—and where a wife could raise her child by the village well.

Sheba gave Noah more pups.

And for a time the family dwelled in that house of peace …

During

Ask the animals, and they will teach you, or the birds of the air, and they will tell you; or speak to the earth, and it will teach you, or let the fish of the sea inform you. Which of these does not know that the hand of the Lord has done this? In his hand is the life of every creature and the breath of all mankind.

Job 12:7–10

Nazareth
✱ ✱ ✱

Some years and many lambs later, Noah and Sheba, the dogs of the stable and of the riverbank, were long in heaven. But their offspring survived to run the streets and houses of the carpenter's village, letting no one pass unknown. The village dogs all came out to greet passing strangers, especially the Roman cavalry, barking at the horses' hooves and the marching cohorts who filled the air with clouds of dust.

The great horses looked down their long noses and warned the dogs in no uncertain terms, "We're bigger, you're smaller. Now keep out of the way."

And the village dogs knew better than to nip the hocks of the great warhorses, but still dashed up and down the line as the Romans tramped through the streets of Nazareth. After all, the dogs knew their business—

"No water here! No water!" they barked over and over. Warhorses had memories longer than their noses so they always remembered the yapping hounds of this village. The big animals whinnied to one another as they passed, "No reason to stop. No water here …" And for years it went on like this, the column of men and horses marching along, the dogs coming out to bark, until the endless stamp of feet and hooves passed the last stone house, the dust settled and the troops wound into the hills.

All village dogs bark, and the dogs of this village were no exception.

Every dog but one: the dog of the carpenter's shop.

The dog called Eden.

Eden's first memory was not her mother's warm belly in the straw, but the hand of the young man upon her head, smelling of sawdust, apricots, cinnamon and fresh hay in a manger. From that first scent Eden always knew whether the young man was close by or beyond the town gate. No distance seemed beyond her reach when it came to his scent.

Sensing him on the barest breeze, knowing where he'd walked and how long he'd tarried by the hem of his sleeve or the sandals on his feet. *Ah yes, by the date trees ... and then talking to a caravan of grain merchants, oxen carts, the cattle dung, the sweat and the sound of a whip*. He had bid the merchants not to beat their animals so—but the hard men ignored him, the echo of their laughter still clung to his robes.

Perhaps that's why Eden didn't chase wildly up and down the narrow dusty street with all the other dogs. She knew where her master was ... so why run about? Instead, she lay under the shop awning out of the noonday heat. Quietly she contemplated those who passed her front door, as sparrows fluttered in the street. The name Eden seemed to fit her as she stared out at the world, her peaceful eyes reflecting that pleasant place everyone knew from ancient legend, but none had ever seen.

She was not a large dog, but not a small one either, and perhaps the most ordinary of the village with her silvery fur and black inquisitive nose. One ear stood up at attention while the other folded down, so it always looked like she was listening. And when both ears stood up straight, Eden became as keen as any hunting hound that ran down rabbits for a living.

Eden

The dog, stretched on out her mat, watched humanity passing before her paws on a thousand errands. Gazing from every point of view: straight on, sideways or even laying on her back, all four feet in the air—the world appearing upside down, as though people walked standing on their heads.

But that did not change the scents of coming and going, one from the Tanner's shed, two from the Oil Seller's row of jars, three from the Carders heavy with the aroma of wool wax as they lugged large roles of yarn to the dyers.

As the afternoon shadows crawled up the plaster walls and the passersby dwindled to a few foot pads, Eden rose to make her rounds of the village, poking her nose into every doorway, looking in on every family and shop. She would pause to listen to the women gossip at the village well where she learned all there was to learn: *Ah, the barber's wife left him, gone back to her sister's again. And did you see that young hussy, that Rachel making eyes at the olive merchant's son and every other man in the street? The rabbi will have something to say about that—*

Finally her rounds ended at the racks of dried-fish sellers on the edge of town, where she watched the weary men herd their flocks home from the fields and orchards. The sheep in their pens mostly talked among themselves, while the shepherds' mongrels were too busy overseeing them to pay her much mind. The shepherds' dogs dismissing her: "*Village dog,*" they snuffed. "Lays around licking her paws all day."

Ah, what did those mutts know? All they did was talk to sheep.

On cool evenings families gathered on their flat roofs sharing food and chatting with their neighbors. The square houses were so close, many ran planks and bridges between the roofs so people could cross without having to go down into the stifling dusty streets. The carpenter's family had built many of these plank bridges between the houses and was often called upon to repair the boards as they loosened and spread.

When the sun set, the village children delighted in running like wild things from house to house along the gangways. And the mothers were forever shouting at them to "slow down, be careful, don't run!" as they bounded from roof to roof. At that time of day Eden came alive, barking at the children, *Don't run! Listen to your mothers! Don't run!*

But children never listen, so Eden followed, nipping at their heels to keep them on the straight and narrow planks. And the children chirruped and laughed but never fell.

In the spring when all the men tilled the fields Eden left her place under the shop's awning and followed the young carpenter and his father into the fields. There she oversaw the work of the seasons as the men sowed the rows and the flocks wandered in search of early grass ... at dusk, finally leading the young master and his father home for the family meal.

At harvest time she helped the men glean and gather the sheaves. During the rainy winter months, Eden sat on her hind legs on the shop's stone doorstep as the street turned to mud.

From the very first, Eden had always understood her master was not like the other men of the village. For unlike the village dogs she always slept in the house instead of with the other animals in a shed or in the street. Her bed was a warm, dry pile of shavings in a corner of the shop, and Eden always had food to eat, for her family shared alike. A clay bowl of water sat by the door—the first vessel in the house to be filled from the village well each day.

From her own safe corner of the shop she watched the young master year in and year out, working his trade. The carpenter's son patiently measured and cut, sanded and planed, fitting piece by piece as he slowly grew from youth to manhood and Eden grew with him. From young pup to wise old dog.... Some winter days her young man left his father's shop to wander alone and Eden followed, walking the hills and pastures under cloudy winds, never more than three steps behind or three ahead. Those times she slept when he slept, woke when he woke, sheltered in the same cloak throughout the night. They drank from the same rocky stream filled with winter's water and ate those same apricots she smelled on his hands when she had first opened her eyes to life.

On one such wander, they came upon a merchant and his camel. The poor beast knelt in the middle of the empty road, refusing to rise, burdened with bales of straw and baskets of goods too heavy even for its strong back. The merchant tugged at the camel's halter, begged and urged it to rise, but the beast refused to budge. The camel's reluctance only infuriated the merchant more, and as Eden and her master came upon them the man raised his whip to strike.

"Help me," the camel said weakly to Eden. "I am old and this straw is too heavy."

When the merchant saw Eden and her master, he fell silent and lowered his crop. The dog watched her master approach the camel. Without speaking he took a rolled carpet from the camel's back and put it aside. The merchant, suddenly afraid, said nothing.

"Does that help?" Eden asked.

"Yes," the camel replied. "But not enough."

Indeed, the rolled carpet was not the only thing her master took from the weary camel. He removed also and set aside a basket of eggs and long bolts of leather. His eyes held the merchant fast; as if to say, *these I shall carry, if you do the same.*

Then waited for the merchant's reply.

The merchantman, now more ashamed than ever, stared at his short crop, as if to wonder, *what are you?* Yet as Eden's master steadfastly gazed, the crop seemed to burn the merchant's hand and he dropped it on the ground. He reached across his camel's back and removed two sacks of grain held together with loops of rope. The loops went over the merchant's head and rested on his shoulders so that he now wore sacks of grain front and back. He looked to his camel, hoping this would be enough.

"Does that help?" Eden asked again.

And the camel replied, "Yes. But not enough."

And this Eden's master seemed to understand. Lastly he removed a dozen strings of dried figs from the camel's back. The figs were strung together with cords. Eden brushed up against his legs and her master laid the strings of figs across her back. The dried fruit was not heavy and Eden wondered what little difference it would make, surely not enough.

And so she asked the camel, "Is *this* enough?"

But the camel did not reply.

Clumsily her master lifted the rug to his own shoulders, then took the basket of eggs in one hand and the long bolts of leather in the other. They were ready to go. Yet the camel did not rise. The merchant stared at his beast still burdened with bales of hay. There were four bales, two on either side. At last he sighed … then removed half the burden, putting two of the four bales by the wayside.

"Perhaps we shall return for them," he said to no one. "Perhaps not …"

And Eden saw the camel's eyes had brightened. It struggled to its knees.

"Yes, it is enough."

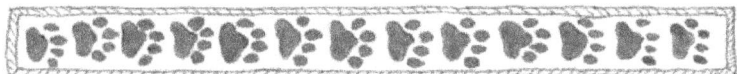

The Essene
✳ ✳ ✳

But more often than not those cool winter days found Eden outside the bare one-room temple where the village prayed. The old teacher with his white goat-like beard taught the young men in that single, dark room what he knew of scrolls and history, bleating in a high, dry voice the story of the known world and the ways of the Almighty's mind:

"I said in mine heart concerning sons of men that they might see that they themselves are beasts. For that which befalleth the sons of men befalleth beasts; as the one dieth, so dieth the other; yea, they have all one breath; so that a man hath no preeminence above a beast: for all *is* vanity."

Yet like the beasts of the field and the beasts of burden in the street, and even like the women of the village, Eden was not allowed inside the temple but huddled out in the street during prayers and teachings. Yet here too, the young master refused to part with her, shunning the room of scholars.

Instead, he sat with her by the open door, listening as the old, dry voice recited the laws and ancient tales. For the young master did not wish to learn alone without his hand upon her head and her head upon his lap, and feared nothing of what the others said when he sat among the women. As ever the dog and man shared his mat, and to anyone who cast a suspicious eye, he told them he could listen just as well in the shadow of the temple wall as inside a bare, dark room.

On more than one occasion, another teacher joined them. This new teacher came from a settlement deep in the wilderness, an outsider, a man of the desert cliffs that overlooked the Dead Sea. On his garments Eden saw the dust of limestone and smelled the scent of caves where men and women lived, staring out over blue saltwater.

The stranger brought his wife and was unlike the people of the village. For though he came out of a harsh place by the lifeless water, his words were softer than those of the rabbi of the town's. And he seemed to smile a little as he left his woman outside with Eden, her master and the others.

Then in the dark, bare temple the Outsider told of his life in the empty desert. "Where we live one cannot separate one grain of sand from the other, and in time we have come to see that any rock can be a temple. Would you sit and not ask your wife to sit beside you? Has she not come as far as you, has she not toiled as you have toiled? Has she not tended you when you were sick, as you tended her with child? Would you not wish her to pray with you as we pray now? Does not God hear those who whisper as well as those who shout? Does he not see those outside the room as those within?"

And then as the students began to murmur in confusion and objection, the teacher from the Dead Sea raised his hand to quiet them—and told the same tale as the old rabbi told, but in a different way:

"To every thing there is a season, and a time to every purpose under the heaven:

A time to be born, and a time to die; a time to plant, and a time to pluck up that which is planted;

A time to kill, and a time to heal; a time to break down, and a time to build up;

A time to weep, and a time to laugh; a time to mourn, and a time to dance;

A time to cast away stones, and a time to gather stones together; a time to embrace, and a time to refrain from embracing;

A time to get, and a time to lose; a time to keep, and a time to cast away;

A time to rend, and a time to sew; a time to keep silence, and a time to speak;

A time to love, and a time to hate; a time of war, and a time of peace."

The teacher from the Dead Sea paused as he left the bare room of the temple and looked down at Eden's master and his dog. The young man rose and bid the man of the desert come under the shop roof for the night before returning with his wife to the settlement of sky and bare rocks. In the house of the carpenter the two spoke long into the night. Eden lay at her master's feet in her soft pile of shavings. She raised her head only once when the man of the desert showed the younger man two small stones he took from his purse. The stones were each of equal weight and size. One stone white, the other black. And the man of the desert asked, "Can you really tell the difference between the two?"

And thereupon he struck one stone against the other and behold, the dark stone was white within and the pale stone black.

"Judge not in haste," the man of the Dead Sea told her master, letting the broken stones fall from his fingers, "unless you know the hidden center of every stone." And he took from his small pouch two more stones, one white, one black, and put them in her master's hands. "The trick is how to find out without breaking them."

Eden sniffed the broken stones that lay on the floor.

Just stones, nothing more.

"Something to think on," the man of the desert told her master.

"Until we meet again."

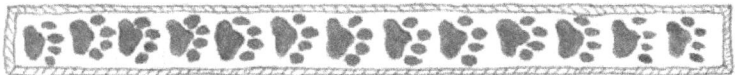

The River
✷ ✷ ✷

Fleeting years and many lambs later, the youth had grown a beard and Eden had grown old. Whiter around the muzzle, and along her paws, her silvery fur all had turned to white.

One day she watched Maryam carefully as the woman of the house packed many things in a traveling sack. Often Maryam would pack her son's midday meal along with his carpenter tools, as he walked to nearby villages to repair a door or a bed. But on that day the woman packed no tools, only the supplies he'd need on the road: flint and tinder, water skin, bread and olives and cheese. And his rolled mat of woven reeds wrapped in his cloak which he carried over his shoulder.

Eden felt the unspoken words of parting between mother and her master. Maryam would miss her son for every day hereon. From the shadow of the carpenter's shop the dog saw Maryam's husband Yosef pause at his workbench and stare silently at the open door. The men had said their good-byes in private and nothing was left to say.

Maryam simply pressed her son's hand to her forehead, then let his hand fall, neither bringing it to her lips nor kissing him farewell. "Come back when you can," was all she said.

But Eden had no intention of watching her master wander

off. That day the dog and her young man walked farther into the green hills than Eden had ever been before. And they did not turn back as night fell, but slept upon the young man's mat of reeds, curled up in their shared cloak till daybreak.

All that next day they marched. The food in the young man's sack vanished bit by bit. By nightfall they were tired and hungry. The man and the dog found shelter in a cluster of rocks by a running rivulet of water that gathered in a small pool no bigger than a few hands wide. Eden lapped gratefully at the stone bowl. And as the sun set Eden stood guard as her master found twisted sticks for a fire.

At first Eden didn't see or smell the stranger's approach. Unannounced, one of the desert people had come out of the wilderness with hardly a sound and no wafting scent on the wind. Once more, the stranger smelled of nothing but sand and stone, his body so thin and gaunt, leaving only the barest essence of a holy man on his threadbare robes. Yet as he sat, she recognized him as the very same who had spoken at the temple, the very same who had spent the night talking in their house and told the story of the stones. The Outsider. The man of the Dead Sea.

So it was not necessary for her master to say, *it's all right. He's one of us.*

Instead he welcomed the man of the desert into their shelter of rocks and bade him sit.

"Indeed, well met."

They lit a fire and shared the last handful of the food from the master's sack. For a long time the three sat in silence, but at length the man of the desert spoke. "Have you been thinking since last we talked? How to discover what lives inside the stone without breaking it?"

Eden looked up at her master, but he did not reply. Instead he loosened his purse strings and removed the two stones, the white and black given that night in their house those fleeting years ago. Her master's fingers turned each over in the light of the fire. Over time each stone had rubbed against the other and in so doing had worn away its outer layer—the dark stone showing its white center and the white stone its dark one.

"Time is the answer," her master said. "Time and familiarity, like friendship. Time and close proximity, like family. Time and close affinity, like marriage. The stones sit in the purse, they rub each other's sides, and *over time* their surface fades and the stones' insides are revealed without breaking."

The Outsider looked in astonishment at his old friend. Then he laughed like a man with twice the belly—the sound rose from their rock shelter into the night.

"I never would have thought of that," he said with a glint in his eye. "After all, it's just a question we ask, *how to see inside without breaking?* No one ever expects an answer!"

And then the two men chuckled, the sound echoing in their shelter, so even the rocks themselves seemed to smile. Their laughter died and quiet returned.

Eden laid down her head and slept her master's hand upon her soft ears. Deep in the night she opened her eyes once more; master's hand was gone. The two men sat by the embers of the fire and spoke in whispers. To Eden they seemed to be speaking only to the stone walls of the shelter, and to the emptiness beyond, but if either the rocks or emptiness heard them Eden did not know. The words themselves she did not fully understand, but she listened carefully just as when she had listened to the man of the desert outside the temple with her master and the women who were not allowed inside.

"A new heart also will I give you, and a new spirit will I put within you: and I will take away the stony heart out of your flesh, and I will give you a heart of flesh."

The man of the desert held a handful of sand in his palm and throughout the rest of the night the two men stared into the cup of his hand as if to count each grain, as they would the souls of men. Eden touched her nose to the man of the desert's palm and snuffed, blowing the grains away.

But neither man seemed upset, her master saying, "So it will be with us."

Eden lay down and closed her eyes, nothing to do but wait out the night. The last thing she heard before falling asleep once more was her master's voice asking:

"Is he still at the river?"

Who might he *be?* Eden wondered. Who knew?

"More gather every day," the man of the desert replied. Then fell silent.

Ah, Eden understood, someone important.

When the sun rose that morning, the dog peeked from the warmth of her master's cloak to find the man of the desert nowhere at hand. The man of no scent had returned to the wilderness leaving behind only the grains of sand once held in his palm, now scattered about the fire pit, back on the ground from whence they came, each grain indistinguishable from the next.

That day's march began in hunger; the stony hills on either side giving neither shelter nor food. The twisted stumps of trees reached for the sky with bare branches, too early in the season for any fruit. As the day lengthened a few pilgrims appeared out of nowhere and many ways seemed to join as one. Their march became a ragged troop, faithful travelers treading a path into the valley of a river. The newcomers gave master and Eden what little food they had brought: a crust of dry bread, a slip of meat, a swallow of water. Another hour passed and the number of pilgrims increased by scores, sending up waves of dust from their tramping feet.

When they reached the river a chill wind blew in from the north under a gray sky. Handfuls of men and women lined the steep, rocky slope along the bank, while those closest to the water's edge gathered together in shivering knots, tugging at their cloaks. Some squatted on boulders while others clung to twisted bushes and the trunks of thin trees whose roots snaked into the water's edge—anything to keep from slipping into the cold current.

The thread of pilgrims, once noisy and talkative on the road, became hushed as they approached the dark, curling water. Even the children among the crowd, always happy to see a dog, were strangely quiet and subdued and refrained from petting Eden. Indeed the whole crowd retreated to frowning silence as newcomers shuffled through breaks in the thickets and closer to the unwelcoming water beyond.

Eden noticed many beggars, the sick, and the hungry. Some wore thin homespun, while the wealthier pilgrims wore thick cloaks. But no matter whether clad in rags or fine wool, heavy care weighed down each pilgrim, unspoken burdens sapping their strength and draining their hope as they shivered in the cold.

Eden sensed deep regret and pain on every leg she passed. Some of those along the riverbank smelled of remorse, others

Eden

of desperation—a scent that overpowered all others. As the pilgrims milled about, the dog could smell their troubles with each leg she saw. And with each breath, another sin. This one beat his wife. That one gave herself to strangers. One failed to mourn a dead father. Another cursed his mother. The sins went on and on ...

Yet none of them dared go into the water. Instead they clung warily to the bushes, and roots along the bank to keep from falling in. Every so often one slipped, soaking his feet, only to scramble away, clinging ever more stubbornly to the rocky shore.

Too fearful, too obstinate, too angry to wash their sins away.

Suddenly Eden looked around. Where was her master?

She had lost her master among the many feet.

In panic Eden ran back and forth among the crowd, frantically snuffing the ground here and there. Trotting from leg to leg. *Are you my master? Are you?* She snuffed the air as deeply as she could, but for once the man's familiar scent was nowhere on the wind. This time all traces of him gone.

"Why run when all you need to do is sit?" a solemn voice asked. Eden stopped in her tracks. By a mound of hay, a calm, gray-faced donkey sat on its haunches, staring moodily over her head.

"I've lost my master!" Eden told him. "Have you seen him?"

The old donkey tucked his nose into his feed, took a mouthful of hay and thoughtfully gazed across the slow river. The long gray face chewed and swallowed, and then at length the donkey cleared his throat.

"Of course—look out into the water. Why fret? Do you think he'd really leave you?" he asked. "Your master stands with *my* master, who stands in the river. Now they both bear the water on cold blue feet."

Eden looked where the long gray nose pointed. The donkey's man stood in the stream. Goatskin pelts barely covered his nakedness as he leaned on a goatherd's crook for support. Eden's master stood there too while the current tugged at his robe, but he bore the cold bravely, standing firmly as the current flowed around his calves—the only pilgrim who dared the river.

Even as Eden watched, the wind sighed and held its breath.

A sound came across the water: the faint bleating of a goat.

Farther out in the stream a tiny goat was swept along by the current. The poor thing struggled to stay afloat, its little gray nose dipping under the water then coming up for air. The creature's feeble cries fell on every ear.

The pilgrims on the bank gasped in dismay, but no one stirred to help the poor thing—more afraid of the river than to see a creature drown. And for a moment Eden caught her master staring at her. So too the goatskin man and now both men stared, as though wanting her to do something. The tiny goat bleated once more and its nose dipped below the surface.

Eden didn't know what came over her.

The dog leapt off the bank, rushing into the stream.

Before the tiny goat floated ten more feet Eden paddled out to the poor struggling thing. One paw cut through the water and then the next, the water rose about her chest, her paws kept paddling and before she knew it she had swum past her master and his friend.

The current was strong, but not so strong she couldn't keep her head above water. The goat looked at her with frightened eyes and its gray nose sank for the last time.

Eden found a good grip on the back of its neck and turned for shore.

This was the hard part, for she was not a youthful dog any longer and her age got the better of her. Eden's legs and shoulders began to fade. The goat in her jaws kicked and fought, gasping every time its nose came up for air, then suddenly went limp, exhausted.

Dead weight, worse than before.

And just when Eden had no more strength left, her burden lessened, the water dripped from her neck, her muzzle and cleared her eyes. Eden still held on to the tiny goat, but her master now held her body above the current. He passed Eden on to another pair of hands, and that pair of hands to yet another, gray goat and white dog passing from willing hands to willing hands, closer and closer to shore.

The pilgrims had braved the river.

In moments, both dog and goat stood on the bank.

Once on firm ground the tiny creature bleated, "Maaa!" shook the water from its flanks; then gamboled from one large boulder to the next. A shepherd and his flock appeared on the crest of a hill, and the nannie bleated back, *"Here!"* The goat beamed in delight and ran to Mama.

Eden watched the lamb run off without even a word of thanks; then shrugged.

Kids ...

When the dog finally shook the water from her fur she doused the old donkey sitting by his mound of hay. The old fellow grumbled, "Must you—?"

But the long gray face didn't seem too put out, almost pleased with himself. "See, I told you your master would never leave."

Eden stared back across the water. Out in the river the ragged, goatskin man spoke into her master's ear, but what he said she couldn't hear. From the rocky shore it seemed the two were long-lost friends. And as the line of people stood in the water waiting to be touched by the strange man, the sun broke through the flat iron of gray clouds and warmed the water's edge.

Before she knew it her master had returned. Eden leapt into his wet arms, and they were both together.

"Your first disciple," the ragged man laughed from where he stood in the river. "Don't lose that one!"

"Yet I have nothing to teach her," her master called back. "She is already perfect." Then to Eden he said, "Come now, let's dry your paws on these sunny rocks. Who knew this riverbank was such an inviting place? There are plenty of warm stones to spare."

The line of people stretched into the water and down the bank. Fear and regret seemed to have vanished from the river's edge. The air grew warmer and Eden heard the sounds of children playing. One or two dogs came out to play as well. Perhaps they'd only been hiding behind the nearest rock, for what dog would abandon its own children?

Eden saw two large golden butterflies fluttering over the water. Tired from her big swim, she laid her head down to sleep, letting the younger dogs play with their kids—unable even to lift her head to watch. Her master sat beside her while the throngs waded into the water to be blessed and the day lengthened into dusk.

That evening the wild man of the water climbed from the stream and stood by the pilgrims' fire warming his limbs until the goatskins dried on his body. Eden and her master sat with him and shared some food from those who remained behind: a handful of dried dates, a loaf of stale bread and river water from a large clay jar.

So tired from saving the drowning lamb, Eden barely ate. As the sun set she slept on the pillow of her master's folded cloak. Faintly she heard the man of the river speaking to her master, words that sounded like a warning.

"You'll find no help out there now. Not where you are going. The final test before you walk among men once more. And if you fail to return no one will know where to find you in the wasteland. No one will remember you existed."

"There is no wasteland," her master replied. "Only lands we've let go to waste." But what those words meant, Eden could not say. Though she heard the hint of a smile in the goatskin man's voice: "A wilderness then."

And felt her master smile in return.

"A garden of stone."

The Wilderness
✸ ✸ ✸

When dawn broke the pilgrims had vanished from the riverside along with all sign of the wild man and his donkey. The two must have departed sometime in the night. As Eden's master prepared to leave, he took with him only what he could carry: a gourd of water, a handful of nuts, a few slices of dried fish.

Eden took a long drink from the river that morning as her master washed his face, a drink of water that seemed to restore her from nose to tail, the strength of puppyhood returning with every swallow. She ran in circles round her master's legs, happy to be alive. The sun rose across the flowing water, its sparkles dazzling their eyes. Dog and man bid farewell to that bright, empty shore, and Eden followed her master into the wilderness.

Though much of her vigor returned, over the course of days the paths they trod weighed down her wagging tail. How many days and nights? Eden could not tell. The dog saw daylight rise and dark night fall about their heads, while the bare earth turned beneath their feet. Grimly they staggered and stumbled through empty canyons of rock.

The handful of nuts and the gourd of water vanished before the first sunset, yet Eden and her master struggled onward. Though by what power their hunger was held at bay neither the man nor animal could say. And though the desert air closed their throats and their salty tongues swelled to fill their mouths, their thirst did not finish them off. They plodded on.

Each day the sun rose through naked towers of stone, and each day they grew thinner in face and muzzle, weary in flesh and breath, yet neither lay down to die. And stranger still, Eden seemed to hear the rocks under their feet speak, whispering in low tones as if to mock them.

"Why are you here?" asked one stone.

"Where are you going?" whispered another.

"Aren't you hungry?" one rock asked.

"Aren't you thirsty?" taunted another.

Eden tried to growl, *can a dog not walk here? Can a man not follow?* But her dry throat made no sound. And as if to tempt her, cold flowing streams filled her mind, visions of rushing water across river stones, dripping combs of wild honey in the trunks of trees, the drowsy hum of many bees, while young lambs bedded down in fields of clover ...

Suddenly Eden realized she'd been standing still for some time, her master no longer walking. She could feel the weariness pour from him. Without a staff for support he sat heavily on a large flat outcropping.

Another creature had joined them in this stark channel of rock.

The newcomer looked very much like a man, but lacked a human smell. No scent of sweat or dirt or even the parched desert came from him, just the stink of ashes and tar, charred bones and crushed hope. He crouched on a narrow ledge in a cleft of rocks and looked down, almost blocking their way. In order to go on they would have to pass under him.

"Are you clean?" the man asked. "Now that you've bathed in

the river?" Eden heard a note of scorn in his voice. As if neither man nor beast could *ever* be clean. She watched her master look up wearily from the stone.

"Clean enough," her master replied, but did not rise, too weak to go around or push on past. Eden felt the two men strive for a moment, their eyes a battle of wills: her master, a man of flesh and blood, against this adversary on the ledge, wearing the skin of a man, a cloak of abysmal deeeps, hiding nothing but emptiness beneath.

"That's a narrow perch on which you sit," her master said at length.

"You're welcome to join me."

"I cannot balance as well as you."

"Well, let us find you some place where you can."

And with that their adversary stood, brushed himself off and turned, leading them to a steep path—unnoticed till now. The hidden path rose upwards into the cliffs. He beckoned and Eden's master began to climb. Not too steep for a man to crawl on hand and knee, nor too steep for Eden. She followed, panting as the barren valley fell away below.

Slower and slower they went, yet ever higher and higher. Finally they stopped to rest on a wide ledge before the mouth of a cave. Eden panted heavily; the air seemed very thin, the stink of tar and ashes filled her nostrils. At some point during their climb night had fallen; the stars shone down, not with majesty and wonder, but with a kind of bitter light, making Eden want to look away.

Once again the two opponents sat in silence. Eden's master held a pebble in his hand and rubbed it with his thumb as though to wear it down, but Eden could not see whether the pebble was white or dark inside.

Their adversary squatted by the cave. Beside him an oil lamp burned.

Yet the flame shed little light, the cave mouth an ugly gash in the side of the mountain. This ledge was not a pleasant place and Eden had no urge to explore further. Even the valley of stones was purer. A scorpion scuttled to the edge of the cave and stared out on the ledge, its pointed tail a crooked finger, searching for something to sting. Another scorpion challenged the first and the two faced off. Their claws clicked, their stingers flicked like poisoned knives, each seeking advantage over the other.

Eden caught her master staring at the two insects. The next moment she saw a glint of laughter in their adversary's eye.

"Can you tell what's inside without breaking them?" he scoffed. Eden's master did not reply. At the cave mouth the scorpions writhed, locked in a death grip, each with a claw about the other's stinger.

Eden saw a flicker of movement in a lump of rock.

A serpent curled on the ledge quietly opened its eye. For several moments it considered the thrashing enemies, each holding a dagger at the other's throat.

The serpent struck. Fangs flashed, jaws snapped and the two scorpions vanished. The serpent curled head to tail once more, nearly invisible again. A lump moved in the serpent's throat as the coiled creature quietly savored victory.

So that was the reason for the glint of laughter. The Hollow Man had known all along what lurked in the dark, ready to devour any creature that crossed its path.

A serpent—far worse than mere insects …

The oil lamp sputtered and went out. Eden saw her master pull his cloak about him, for the air had grown cold. But then thinking better, he took it off, folding his cloak to make a pad for her. The stars overhead wheeled silently across the sky and the three silent figures sat before the cave mouth under a moving dome of endless night.

How much time passed Eden did not know.

When she gazed across the ledge again their adversary held the serpent in his lap. The snake was dead and the Hollow Man had skinned it, laying bare its flesh.

"One of the scorpions must have struck on the way down," he said softly. "Or maybe both did. He ate too fast. Anyway, this gives us meat."

A strip of snake dangled in his fingers and he tossed the dainty before Eden's nose. The aroma filled her nostrils, not evil but delicious, the finest meat she'd ever smelled. And a hunger rose in her, a hunger unlike any she had ever known.

"Go on, take it," the Hollow Man said. "We can't go on like this forever."

Eden's will began to weaken, her mouth watering for the first time in god knows when. But she knew if she took this slip of meat she would no longer be her master's friend and protector, but this *creature's* creature sitting across in the dark. He would own her, possess her, she'd become *his* alone. Just when she thought she would succumb, when she began to crawl on her belly for a taste ... her master's soft voice held her close.

"Why not?" he asked. "Why can't we go on forever?"

The Hollow Man seemed taken aback; he had not foreseen this turn.

But then he slyly turned her master's mind back on itself, pointing toward the ledge and the currents of air rising into their faces.

"Prove it. Take that step ... and I'll follow *you*."

Her master looked over the ledge into the stony abyss, an endless fall. Eden joined him, poking her nose over, but his arm blocked her from going farther. They retreated from the edge.

"Follow whomever you wish," she heard her master say, "but by your choice we shall know you." And with that Eden's hunger suddenly vanished. She no longer wanted that bit of meat that had seemed so delicious only a moment before. She sat by her master's feet and felt his hand upon her shoulder. "You have free will," her master told the Hollow Man. "*He* gave you that. But you cannot have mine."

The creature sitting in the dark did not seem vexed. He shrugged and gazed out across the open abyss.

Suddenly a vision seemed to grow from the depths of the emptiness. The very world itself lay like an endless carpet. Eden had no idea the world could be this big, this grand: open deserts, snow-clad mountains, lakes and forests, a thousand castles, a thousand palaces, a thousand streets and markets, ports and harbors overflowing with the goods of every land, nation upon nation, stretching beyond sight and out of mind.

A sea of faces lifted upward all begging to worship those sitting on the ledge: the faces of the living, the faces of the dead, even the faces of all those yet to be born like eager spirits clamoring in adoration of those three figures perched above. The nameless throngs would slave for them, die for them, kill for them, make monuments to their magnificence, burn offerings and sacrifice the lambs of the world.

The horizons of all Eden had ever known shrank to a paw print in the sand. The little village, the dried-fish seller, the clamoring children on the rooftops, the men in the fields and the sheep in the orchards, became the merest speck on this lush carpet of humanity and beasts and all their works.

The very world.

Offered to her master, offered to her ...

And she heard the silky voice of their adversary bargaining all for all, "Will this not make you follow me? For what is mine shall be yours and more besides ..."

Eden looked into the black void below, then into the black void above, and the stars stopped wheeling in their endless orbits. "Get away!" she tried to growl, but she found her jaws locked together, the cliff fading from her eyes. The stars blinked out one by one. The abyss opened at her feet.

And she fell, falling, falling and knew no more.

Eden awoke at the base of the cliff in the pit of the barren valley as if she had never been up high. The stones no longer mocked her, but lay mute on every side. She lay on her side in the dark, tongue swollen with thirst, eyes crusted with salt. The adversary of the high place was nowhere to be seen, his scorpions and serpent only a memory.

The man lay beside her, exhausted, beaten. His chest slowly rose and fell, he barely breathed. And then to make things worse, Eden realized they were not alone.

Three hyenas had padded to the lip of the dell and stared down. Their lips peeled back from their teeth and when they laughed at her, Eden's bones grew cold.

Nor did they wait to attack. Two came on as one, forcing her against the cliff, and the third went for the man on the ground. That one tore at her master's cloak, and in the darkness Eden saw a flash of naked skin. Eden didn't think—she ripped through the two hyenas, snapping one in the face and the other on the snout. The third tearing her master's cloak yelped when her teeth clamped on his neck.

But one dog against three couldn't last for long. The hyenas cornered Eden again, and as each lunged, she'd snap, then snap at the next and the next. Panting, she finally missed one and he clamped on her ear. A flash of pain filled her head and blood ran over her eyes.

Even so she struck out blindly, but the hyenas were just playing with her now. There was nothing to stop them from tearing at the prostrate man. He groaned but could not rise.

This was the end then ...

Eden felt it in her heart. The man's hand held Eden close to him.

All she could do was lie on her master, just lie on him and let the devils get her too—

The three hyenas grinned at her one last time.

Blood speckled her white fur.

For a moment they hesitated before the final go. Why stop now?

A faint sound came to Eden's torn ear.

The sound of little bells jangled sweetly in the air. Their brassy chimes filled the narrow ravine. Three large rams with bells about their necks bounded across the stones, followed by three fat ewes. The ewes circled Eden and her master, while the rams with their great horns went straight at the grinning hyenas. With a thud of horn on hide and three terrified yelps, the devils fled, limping as they ran.

And the sound of tiny brass bells echoed off the cliff face.

They were saved.

Eden felt someone licking the blood from her face and the cut on her ear. At once she recognized the young goat from the river, the kid's little gray muzzle nuzzled her face. *You saved me, you saved me,* the little animal whispered. Goodness gracious—a goat among the sheep, and Eden almost laughed, but her throat was too dry. A great udder appeared in front of her nose and she suckled like a pup again. And when the sun rose in the narrow ravine her master was sitting up, breathing easier now, drinking milk from that empty gourd. No rams. No hyenas. No little kid.

And when Eden touched her mangled ear with her paw, yes, a scrap of white fur was gone, but the flesh had knit closed, fresh as new.

A Wedding
✷ ✷ ✷

The followers did not come all at once, but as drops of rain at the head of a storm, first one, then another, and then another ...

Eden stood by the riverbank once more. Her master had returned to speak and a few people, recently touched by the water, stayed to listen and to dry themselves by the campfires. The dog felt her master's mind, his hopes and fears like an aura all on its own. He needed to do many things. But he could not do it all alone. Much would he say, and many would listen— *but he needed men to help him.* Nearby, the wild man's donkey roused himself from his mound of fodder and stood quietly by, listening as her master's voice rose and fell.

At last the donkey spoke, "No one thought you'd ever come back."

Eden thought of the hunger and thirst, the mocking stones. "Me either."

"What did you see?"

She thought of the strange, empty man and his evil creatures. *What to say? We met the man at the end of the world, he tried to tempt us.* No ... instead she told the donkey:

"Hyenas and goats."

The donkey nodded gravely. "That sounds a lot like here." He shook his head and shifted his ears. "What did you learn?"

"I learned the world is broad and wide, bigger than this riverbank, bigger than our village, bigger than even the wasteland."

The donkey grew silent, considering Eden's words. At last he said, "I would like to see this world you speak of."

"Won't your master miss you?" Eden asked the donkey.

Again, the old donkey pondered her words.

"No," he finally told her. "The man of the river carries his own burdens."

Eden looked at the man of the river standing by the campfire, listening with the others. He leaned on his staff for support, weary in body and mind, but his face and eyes in the firelight seemed lit within just by standing in her master's circle.

"You'll have to leave your mound of hay behind," Eden told the gray-faced donkey.

"At least I can forage by the side of the road. But what of you?"

Eden looked at the knot of people gathered by their campfires. Her master's words rose and fell on their upturned faces. "So far I have never starved," she told the donkey. "There is food by the roadside for me as well. Through thick and thin, somehow the world provides."

That settled matters. So in the end the donkey joined them.

They journeyed north towards the great lake. And yes, the world was broad and wide, and as each league passed they found food where it appeared and neither dog nor donkey went hungry. They kept to the river where grass grew and in the swampy places they rooted about in hoopoes' nests and stole pelican eggs. In other places, her master swept fish out of eddies with his hands to flap on the rocks, cooking them on hot coals.

At night he spoke by the campfires of those who journeyed, and food was shared even when there was little to go around.

But somehow, miraculously, neither man nor animal starved. And as the sun rose each day, Eden and the donkey looked ahead with fresh eyes.

After a few nights, the two animals and their master were no longer alone, as newcomers had joined them. These were also travelers who stopped to listen by the campfire, only to awake the next dawn wishing to follow the sound of the master's words and see the wider world. Without even an invitation the newcomers abandoned their personal journeys, as if joining paths with a dog, a donkey and a total stranger were the most natural thing in the world. But where this stranger, his dog and the donkey would lead them—where the travelers were bound or what they would find—no one knew.

What they *did* know was *expectation* in dawn's first breath, free of fear, free of doubt—as though this trek past nameless hills and hovels, this march along the river, heralded some great event.

Perhaps this was when the mice of the field began to mark their passing, peeking through the tufts of grass at the travelers' padding feet, then murmuring mouse to mouse—*behold! Behold!*

A stranger who walks from place to place, needing nothing to sustain him but a few fish from the river, a little water and the arc of heaven over his head as shelter for the night. *Clearly, this is no ordinary man*, the mice whispered among themselves, *nor those who follow him. Why do they follow? What can they hope to gain? And what purpose served?* No mouse could say.

After many leagues the stranger's journey brought him to the shore of a wide lake, where on a hill nearby a great celebration was being held.

Eden

As the companions trudged up the dusty road, they learned the celebration was a wedding. The revelers welcomed them into the circle of tents.

At first the travelers rested on the edges of the party asking neither for food nor drink. But after a few moments Eden sensed a familiar smell, the family-smell. There on the ground, a footprint! The scent of sawdust and wooden-handled tools, the scent of sharp chisels and the sweat of working—yes, she knew it now! A member of her master's family—her master's mother! And Eden put a familiar face with that familiar smell.

The woman from the carpenter's shop emerged from the crowd to welcome them and Eden rushed to greet her. And once more that familiar hand stroked Eden's ears as it had all those years she had lain in front of the shop watching the world pass by.

Soon the platters and jars were passed around and the travelers ate and drank their fill, wrapped in the embrace of the wedding party as if they had always belonged. The gray-faced donkey found a mound of hay behind a tent, and Eden a great lamb shank discarded by the fire pit with thick shreds of meat clinging to it.

But as the day drew on and more and more people came to join the party of tents, the servants were called again and again to fill every jar and every cup and every plate. And as greater numbers joined the celebration, the platters of food began to thin and the jars began to drain, and Eden saw the worried looks on the faces of the elders. Their dismay grew as the servants returned with less and less food, and the wine jars lay empty on their sides.

The donkey took his nose out of the mound of hay.

"Perhaps we should leave now and not burden this family further," he said to Eden.

Then she saw the carpenter's woman speak into her master's ear, urging her son to do something, take some action, relieve the elders' distress at the lack of food and drink. But her master merely shook his head, refusing to intervene, even as the next platter passed to him was nearly bare. Yet his mother persisted, convinced her son could do something.

Then one of the new companions suddenly rose, caught up in this pressing moment. He stood looking at the carpenter's woman, and also their master, and waved his arms at the crowd now combing the platters and jars for more. His voice rose in urgency, as if it would make what he said more true:

"The burden is in the fear of want, Master. Banish want and we banish fear. We banish violence and anger and strife."

The carpenter's woman left her son's side. Gently she brought the passionate companion back to his seat with the calm hands Eden knew so well. And with one glance their master bid his new friend be silent, as if this were no place or time for anxious words or speeches.

The donkey dipped his long gray nose, whispering to Eden:

"No one can banish fear. And no man can banish want. We are born in want and die in fear. That is the way of it."

Eden thought about the donkey's words and saw her master sigh, then make up his mind. He rose from their group and went to a servant, where he picked through the remains on that last platter. Then her master went to another servant and peered deeply into an empty jar. A few words were exchanged between her master and the servants, but none that seemed to satisfy the moment.

The servants muttered and took both jar and platter away, hopelessly discouraged on an errand for more.

"Perhaps the best we can do," Eden told the donkey, "is not let want or fear fill the life we've been given."

She had been watching an old dog for some time now. The ancient fellow lay in the shadow of a tent flap, so worn and tired he could barely raise his head. But his eyes were bright, and Eden knew if he had been just a little younger he would have come over to play. Before she knew what she did, she took her meaty bone and instead of snarling over it alone, she brought it to the old one and set it by his paws.

And the guests stared in wonder, for no dog acted thus. And they forgot their fear of emptiness and want. And as the jars were passed around, no man or woman could tell where the sweet drink began and the water of the lake ended, or where the full platter of lamb began and devoured bones gave out. They drank from the jars and it went into their hearts like wine, their spirits lifted and voices sang. Even as they reached onto each platter of food, whether they found discarded shreds, gristle or just a grain of rice, no one went hungry.

The travelers left that evening, not wishing to overstay their welcome, but word of this amazing feast, how dog fed dog and none went hungry or thirsty, preceded the companions on the tails of mice scampering over rocks and blades of grass. Eden could hear them whisper as they ran—*Behold! We have witnessed! We have seen!*

As the sun set, fishermen beached their boats on the shore, furled their sails and hung their nets to dry. The dark fell over the lake and Eden saw brick furnaces along the strand smelting metal. Bellows blew the charcoal white, while little glowing rivers of iron dripped into catch basins like angry, writhing snakes. The clank and spark of hammered iron echoed across the water as the companions walked into the night. Men were making swords.

The wheezing furnaces and clanking anvils faded behind them. They passed fields on either side of the road, long abandoned. A wind blew across the pasture rattling dry stalks like idle chatter and the fallow earth gave off the scent of neglect.

Eden snuffed the air, but all she sensed was emptiness.

Back on the shore men made swords, swords aplenty, but here there was no one to plow. Furrows but no shoots, long rows of weeds but nothing sown. On the rise of a hill she saw a lonely plow leaning on its side, the metal plowshare taken for the smithies' furnaces below.

"Where is the plowman?" Eden asked. "A plow without a plowman, a plow without a blade and many swords below.... Where is the plowman?"

The old gray donkey shook his head. He did not know.

That night the companions sat about their campfire but did not speak. Eden could feel their loss of words. The clank of hammer on anvil had silenced them. The wind sighing over forsaken fields had silenced them. Mute stars in the cloak of night silenced them, leaving both man and animal alone in their thoughts till dawn. And the mice watched in silence from the surrounding fields.

Another two days' march passed without event.

Until at last they reached the gates of a large city.

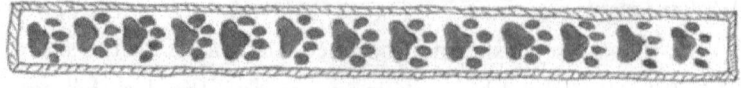

Judas
✳ ✳ ✳

Neither Eden nor the donkey knew so many people and animals could live together. The people of this place seemed to be falling off their flat rooftops along with their huffy roosters—fussy birds who crowed, "More people, send them away! More people, send them away!"

The companions kept close in the narrow, crowded streets, not wanting to be separated or lost. Clumsy oafs stepped on Eden's paws and she yelped, strangers shoved the donkey and whipped his behind even though they didn't know him. "Oh this place is awful," the gray donkey brayed. "Take us away, let us leave."

But their master knew his destination. The great temple. And he bid the animals stay outside, leaving them in the care of his companions.

"Wait here."

He approached the temple gates, swept aside a corner of the bright curtains and passed into the courtyard. A handful of men milled about in the busy street in the muted shadow of the temple walls. Eden and the donkey peered through the colorful swaying linen, glimpsing stalls and merchants crowding the enclosure. Inside, the temple was as busy as the street, while outside one companion paced anxiously before the temple wall, another wrung his hands gaping at the noisy throngs and yet a third clutched the donkey's halter with one hand and clutched the dog with the other.

Suddenly a great commotion erupted from the enclosure. Eden could hear her master shouting. She had never heard him so angry. He was shouting at the people inside the temple courtyard. Her master wanted the merchants be gone from the holy place. He tore at them with a fury Eden had never known.

Tent poles fell, the merchants began to cry and then shriek in rage.

Chaos reigned.

The cracking of broken pots rang off the stone walls. A bright cascade of coins jingled in the air and tinkled like a thousand bells as they hit the paving stones. A covey of doves exploded overhead, circled the compound and flew in a hundred directions. By the temple gate twenty lambs ran willy-nilly through the curtains, past Eden and the donkey, bleating, "We're free! We're free!"

The two animals looked at each other and laughed. The lambs' owner stumbled past them with a switch, cursing anyone who stood in his way.

"Free until they're caught again," the donkey said.

Last of all their master appeared, and strode from the temple compound without looking back. In full rage, merchants from the enclosure threw bruised fruit at him, striking his shoulders, staining his cloak. His companions leapt to shield him, standing at their master's back as the wrathful traders cursed and shouted. But the companions' stern faces kept them at a distance. The angry stall owners and money changers dared not come closer.

A single coin rolled out the temple gate following their master's footsteps, then fell on its side and lay still.

At once three beggars from the street pounced on it. They snarled and tore at each other's rags for possession of the single coin. Eden and the donkey were shoved against the temple wall, while their master looked at the desperate men in pity. The coin was snatched from hand to hand until one of the beggars dropped it and it rolled off once more. The three scrabbled in the gutter, but the precious coin rolled into a drain by the grated curb and vanished down a sewer.

The pitiful ragged souls stood about the hole in the street and began to weep.

Silently Eden's master removed his coat and handed it to one of them.

"Sell this or wear it," he said.

The three beggars paused, uncertain what to do. The stall owners and money changers whispered among themselves, more confused than angry now.

Three beggars, but with only one coat between them …

Their master tightened his belt about his robe and gazed at his companions with a question in his eyes. Had they nothing to offer too?

A moment passed, and in those few seconds the companions understood, not needing to be told. They too offered what little they possessed. An old woolen cloak to one ragged man, an extra pair of sandals to another, a threadbare shirt to a third, worn but clean …

The stall owners and money changers, the traders and merchants, huddled together in the shadow of the temple curtains, their anger gone. Then one by one each turned from what they witnessed in the street and returned to the enclosure.

All except for one among them, a slight man with red hair and hard eyes, who found something of his own to give. He seemed both fascinated and yet ashamed. Cautiously, he fished a few dull coins from his leather purse, putting coppers into the palm of each beggar.

And before the day ended the travelers found yet another who wished to follow.

His name was Judas.

The companions left the city that very hour. In the hills to the east Eden heard the tinkle of silvery bells, not wild rams this time, but the temple lambs. From out of nowhere the fleeing sheep appeared; a noisy confused mob of curious faces. So the lucky things had slipped the herdsman's crook after all:

"Who are you? Where are you going?" the lambs bleated all at once. "Can we come too? Are you our masters now? What are your names?"

The lambs' tiny voices bewildered Eden's ears.

"Children, don't talk all at once!" the dog told them. "And straighten up that line," which they did, one by one and two by two. After a moment, the herd came to heel, following the dog and the donkey as if they'd always belonged there.

"We're not going to have you wandering all over the road and getting underfoot!" Eden scolded.

And the little lambs bleated back, "Yes, Miss. Yes, we will. But where are we going and what kind of dog are you?"

Eden fell silent. Indeed what kind of dog *was* she? The old village dog, her master's companion, nameless traveler.... She glanced at the donkey and realized she didn't even know his name. The long gray nose looked down at her as if he read her thoughts.

"I have the same name every donkey is given. What they shout at you from the day you're born. Mostly, *Get Going!* Or *Dammit, Get Going!* But when I came to the man in the river, my burdens were lifted, I sat on the bank eating hay as you found me, and no one shouted at me anymore."

"Then let us find you a new name," Eden told him. She looked over the half dozen lambs, trotting after them. "What do you children think? What shall we name our big, strong friend?"

For a moment the lambs padded on in silence, then shrilled as a chorus all at once, "Samson! We'll call him Samson, because he's so big and strong and his mane is so stiff and spikey." Then all at once, "Samson! Samson! Samson!"

When the chorus died down, Eden looked at their large companion. The old gray donkey thought seriously. Then nodded his ruff:

"Better than *Dammit*," the donkey said. "Samson is good."

He cleared his throat. "And the children have a point. Where *are* we going?"

As it turned out, back to that wide lake where the companions had joined the wedding feast, where Eden had shared her bone with the dog too old to fight for it and where Eden's master had seen that no one went hungry. The place where clay furnaces smelted ore into iron and smithies pounded iron into swords, a great wide sea of fishermen, boats and nets, and fishtails on the shore.

But for Eden that single destination didn't answer the question.

Where *were* they going? Nowhere and everywhere. Across

the lengths of the land they wandered, always on the move, never tarrying for long, their master speaking to any who would listen. Samson the donkey plodded along on stoic hooves, the little lambs trotted behind without complaint. Stranger still, the lambs seemed to stay little lambs and not grow any older, and the donkey's hide grew lustrous, his face no longer gray. Eden ran all day to catch the wayward little ones, but never seemed to tire.

While the dog's sharp eyes made sure no lamb strayed.

And none of them ever did.

While the mice in the fields gossiped among themselves. *Look at her run! She's so fast, she's so strong, she's so smart!*

Night devoured day and day banished night. Their road seemed an endless march, and Eden watched the crowds gather at her master's feet with every league. When the companions paused to rest or talk, she never wandered far from his side. Did he love her the same as before? As when the two of them struggled with that Hollow Man on the ledge, or lay broken down below, waiting for the end?

Eden did not know.

Like the two worn stones, the black and the white that had rubbed till their insides showed, Eden and her master were there for all to see. When she came near him, his hand reached for her, and when he spoke he drew her close so she might sit beside him and listen with the others. And well-being seemed to flow from him, filling Eden with a kind of light, for which she knew no name ...

As for the companions, they treated Eden as one of their own, and she knew each man by his scent. Mostly they were clean scents, not the stench of labor and worry. For walking purified you, as if each step you took shed a bit of your troubles by the wayside, cleansing each man the farther he traveled.

But the one named Judas was different from the others, and the companions treated him so. At first he stood out because he gave his money to the beggars at the temple walls. Despite the gift of a few copper coins, or perhaps because of it, the others let him carry their common purse, trusting him to hold what little they possessed. A few meager coins: mostly coppers, one silver, but no gold.

Later, he stood out because he acted differently, withdrawing from the others when they rested for the night. But what could Eden tell? He smelled of little more than human sweat and a dusty road. Yet the scent of sadness and doubt clung to his robes and Eden often went to him, letting the man stroke her ears as they kept watch at night. Not a bad man, but he shrank from every nighttime shadow, dreaded every turn in the road on the next day's march. And Judas often walked alone.

Samson noticed it too, coming to the man's side when Judas retreated into periods of heavy thought. Then he mumbled to himself as though struggling with an invisible foe, as if a foreign spirit possessed his mind. Muttering phrases and broken sentences even as Eden walked on one side, Samson the donkey on the other. The animals never truly understood what Judas said, but they let him ramble on, every now and then croaking:

"Stop it!"

"Get out!"

Then Judas would pause by the roadside to scratch under his cloak, searching his clothes, examining his arms and legs as if they were crawling with mites. Eden and Samson felt the burden of an extra mind constantly tormenting him, as he argued with some creature who wasn't there. Muttering:

"Get away."
"I won't!"
"You can't make me!"

For their part the animals let Judas talk, letting the troubled man unravel the knots within until he fell silent of his own accord. Of course the companions noticed too and Eden's master most of all, but no one thought badly of Judas. Or wished him cast from their circle. He was one among friends. And over countless miles the man's endless arguments with himself seemed to lessen. But whether Judas calmed the storms within or smothered them by force of will, no one could say.

Signs and Wonders
✳ ✳ ✳

Now a time of wonder changed all things known as Eden's master drew the improbable from the hopeless like thread off a spool. By the touch of his hand, a glance, the flicker of a smile ... he altered what could never be to that which stood beyond a shadow of a doubt. The companions rubbed their eyes and gaped like fools.

While the animals—

Eden, Samson and the lambs, being innocent of all corruption—

Accepted everything as it happened.

For like the mice who crouched behind every rock and gnarled root, the animals needed no herald to tell them what they saw with their own eyes. And as the travelers walked from hovel to hut, from meadow to orchard, the dog, the donkey and the lambs watched the mice come out of hiding. Lining the roadside the little creatures waved green blades of grass as the companions passed. For countless throngs and tribes from every pasture had heard of the strange tidings, the tale of the many strangers who feasted, the tale of the lambs set free ... and the mice cried in their high voices, "We have heard of you from afar, from our cousins in every ditch and field."

Then the many mice laid the thin green spears on the dusty

roadway so all might tread on soft ground. Eden looked boldly at them and Samson stiffened his ears, both animals amazed that so many had heard of them, that so many noticed.

The lambs snuffled shyly, "It wasn't our doing, not us, not us …" but still pleased to be praised simply for walking by, murmuring lamb to lamb, "What admirable mice there are in the world. Do you think they are right? Perhaps we *are* amazing!"

Even a fox paused on his endless hunt for dinner, ignored the mice at his feet and wondered out loud, "Can it all be true? These signs, these marvels?"

"Join us and see," Eden called out to him.

But the fox, perplexed, shook his head and muttered, "No, I think not. I will have to ponder what this means. Though I shall not walk with you today, I shall never be far."

Of the many miracles known and counted, the animals saw only a portion. So some great works were forgotten, while those remembered lived on as spoken tales the animals may not have heard and in scrolls the animals could not read. But as Eden and the companions marched from hill to vale, or rested beside tree or stream, no ailing creature went untouched, no sick thing ignored if it came before their master's feet.

In all that time three great moments stood out in Eden's mind.

They had come to a village at dusk with nowhere to sleep.

Nothing unusual in this …

They often wandered into places and were rarely turned away during the day. For their master's name had spread far and wide, going before him like those blades of grass waved by the field mice. But people closed their doors against strangers after dark, thus the night was no time to come begging for shelter.

This place was much like Eden's own town of the carpenter's

shop. On the outskirts date palms and pastures, sheep and cattle in pens … then narrow streets and the houses so close together, ramps and gangways sprang from roof to roof. Just like home.

The companions and the animals stopped at the shop of a potter, his house attached to a shed. On shelves sat row upon row of fired vessels. The potter's wheel was still, a damp cloth over a lump of clay, and in the depths of the dark a cold kiln no ember burned.

The jostling lambs, the dog and the donkey crowded together in the street. Eden stood under Samson's broad belly to keep from getting stepped on. One of the lambs bumped into a clay pot by the potter's doorstep, tipping it over. The crack of broken clay rang off the street stones.

"We'll have to pay for that!" Eden snapped at the lambs. "Behave yourselves! No pushing!"

The lambs hung their heads, ashamed, while the companions rushed to pick up the broken pot shards. They looked to Judas in dismay and feared for the meager coins in their common purse. Clay pots weren't free; how could they afford this? Such a pot would cost more than a few coppers.

Suspicious eyes stared out at them from half-open doors and windows along the street, but no voice rose in anger from inside the potter's house.

Two small candles burned within.

A child lay on a low bed. Her father, the potter, stood in a dark corner, while her mother knelt by the bedside. The woman didn't look up but quietly wrung her hands and grasped the wooden leg of the bed, as if by stroking the bed's leg the child might come alive again. Eden saw a little girl, her eyes rolled upwards showing the whites. At her feet curled another dog, not unlike Eden except you could see the creature's eyes alert, watching for anyone's approach.

The companions' curious faces crowded at the door.

The watchful dog uncurled, bared its lips, snarling, "Get away …"

Then lay across the child's legs, guarding her.

The child's father came out of the shadow and went to the door where the companion called Judas offered him coins from the common purse for the broken clay pot. At first the potter stared at the open palm, but didn't seem to understand what the coins were for, or didn't care. Instead, the potter folded Judas' fingers closed, imploring:

"Please, please ask your master," the potter whispered in a broken voice. "Ask him for me. I beg you. Ask him. There must be something he can do."

Judas listened carefully as the father told how his child had hurt herself, and then tucked the purse in his belt and went to where their master stood in the street. Eden's sharp ears heard every word.

"The little girl and the dog were running with the other children, from house to house as they always do. One of the gangways slipped from a roof. She and the dog fell into a hay cart. She fell with the dog clutched in her arms, but the wind was knocked from her. Now she cannot wake and the dog will not leave her bed." The other companions who had gathered close murmured among themselves considering what could be done, and the animals crowded at the doorway.

Samson poked his long nose into the potter's house, the lambs shuffling about bleating, "Let us see! Let us see!" The donkey looked down with serious ears. "If you can't grow up, the least you can do is be quiet."

"Hush now," Eden shushed the noisy things, "And go into the street before I growl."

The lambs turned away in disappointment. "Aw ... we want to see."

"There's nothing to look at yet. Go be good," Eden told them. Her eyes dwelt on the dog on the bed. She knew that look. *Approach and die. Be warned.*

The potter gazed over everyone in the crowded street and shook his head in dismay. He had not enough room inside to invite them in, but didn't want anyone to leave. Would their master try to help? Eden did not know.

At last, her master said to the potter:

"We shall wait with you."

Then to Judas and the others:

"Let us remain here in the street. Let us rest by the open door where our thoughts and prayers can be heard by all who listen from above and those who listen from within."

The companions began to complain. The street was too hard, the night too cold, with nothing but a house wall to rest their heads on. They'd even given away their cloaks in the last town, and if they paid for the broken pot there'd be no money even for a crust of bread in the morning.

The animals grumbled too, even though they knew discomfort more than people. Each of them looked for places to bed down as the dark came on. Samson was too big in the narrow street to find a comfortable spot, complaining to anyone who would listen, "No grass, no water ... nowhere to lie down. I want a stable with a manger. There must be one nearby." Craning his neck and trying to look around corners. "Do you see a stable down there? Let's find a manger."

And the lambs were no better, crying as one, "What about us? What about us? Doesn't anyone care about us?"

"Shush, all of you!" Eden scolded. "You've been colder before, hungrier before, and no one says you have to stay!"

Ashamed, the young lambs looked down at their hooves. They huddled by the nearest wall, making do as best they could. Samson wedged down in a tight corner, beside them. The donkey dipped his ears, "And no doubt I'll be colder and hungrier again. Certainly by tomorrow morning if not sooner!" he grumbled.

The lambs, hopeful as always, bleated, "But look how cozy it is now!"

Eden lay on the potter's doorstep so she could watch both inside and out. The dog on the child's bed glared at her with dangerous eyes, pressing his body across the child's legs—but she ignored him. Instead she stared at her master and the one named Judas who seemed to have forgotten everything around them, the two men silently gazed into each other's eyes as the rest slept.

Murmured prayers hung in the air as the night closed in.

The potter sat at the open door as well, the girl's mother curled by the foot of the bed, and both nodded in restless sleep, their heads to their breasts. The night lengthened ...

Eden suddenly opened her eyes. She must have fallen asleep.

Her master stood in the doorway looking in. The potter and the potter's wife lifted their heads in alarm and the dog on the child's bed bared its teeth. *Be warned.*

Eden partially rose an inch from her place on the doorstep and on all four paws crawled on her belly into the room. She barely moved her legs, head down, ears back—still the dog on the bed growled, low and long.

As Eden lay on the floor inside the room, she rolled on her side. She could feel the fear inside the other dog's mind. His memory of the sudden fall from the ramp: the terror in the child's arms as they fell through the air, the brutal thump when they landed in the hay cart. The dog on the bed began to tremble—

"It's over now," Eden told him. "You're not going to fall again. No one is going to hurt you. Let my master touch your girl. Let me come close and kiss your ear."

"Why?" the dog growled low in his throat, his paws pressing the child's legs. "Why do they never listen? I told her not to run on the ramps! I always tell them that!"

Eden crawled an inch closer. "They never listen. Not to us. Not even to each other."

The dog on the bed stopped trembling. Something in Eden's voice touched him in a good way. And his ears perked to listen more. "They *should* listen."

"Yes, they should," Eden said. "Let us both show we can listen even when they don't. Listen to me now." She crawled closer. Her nose just under the bed. "Can I sit up instead of crawl? Can I kiss your ear?" The angry dog said nothing.

Eden laid her head on the edge of the bed. The angry dog put his head beside her, but did not move his paws.

"My nose. You can kiss my nose."

Eden nuzzled the angry dog's nose. He took a deep breath and sighed.

Her master stood over the bed and knelt by the child, and the angry dog did not object. Softly her master began to speak into the little girl's ear, so softly Eden couldn't catch what words he spoke, just that he was telling the little girl how much her parents loved her, how much they wanted her to get better, how much they wanted to see her open her eyes again ...

Her master's soft whispers went on for a long time. His voice rose and fell, reminding Eden of that time when he had counted the grains of sand in the Desert Man's hand. And the angry dog's eyes had closed to tight slits. He was beginning to sleep, the first sleep since their fall from the gangway, the first sleep in a long time.

"I'm going to kiss your girl," Eden murmured.

And the angry dog murmured, "All right. All right. Just let me sleep a bit."

Eden's nose nuzzled the little girl's ear, "Everyone loves you. Wake up. We're all here."

The little girl struggled in her dark sleep and her eyes fluttered.

Eden returned to the angry dog. "Why don't you kiss her? She'd like it, if it was you instead of me."

The sleeping dog opened his eyes, rose from the foot of the bed and stretched. Carefully he padded up to the child's face and nuzzled her, saying, "I'm here now. I'm here."

Eden held her breath.

The girl's eyes fluttered again. In a corner of the room, the potter clutched his wife and she pressed a hand to her mouth to keep from crying out. Then fell to their master's knees to kiss his hand. The lambs had joined Samson and the crowd of onlookers at the door. Many heads and faces looked in, worried faces, gaping mouths, eyes wide in awe and wonder.

At the doorway with the others, Judas didn't know what to make of what he saw.

Fear and doubt and longing fought a silent battle. Could he really believe his lying eyes? Shaken, he turned his face away ...

but then slowly stared again, as if he could not bear to lose this moment. Yes, no denying the child had woken from her dark sleep.

And the girl cried.

As though for the first time.

The name of this man spread like birds through a field of wheat, the word of his coming flying on sparrows' wings, swooping over the stalks.

They came to him in flocks.

Out from their homes and off their fields to greet the companions even miles from the nearest town, to offer them food or drink with little enough of their own to spare. Total strangers welcomed the companions with firewood or shelter for the night if only to sit and hear a few of their master's words. For their master stopped in many places to speak, sitting upon rock or fallen tree while those who gathered listened, not only to his words but to the sound of his voice, which sustained them in ways food had never done.

During these times Eden sat with the one called Judas, who held her in his lap as her master's words rose and fell and people listened and learned. Some learned to pray for the first time, others to love for the first time and yet others to forgive. Many lessons were given and many remembered, but what Eden remembered most clearly were the lambs quietly grazing among the gathered, and Samson the donkey silently swishing his tail. Judas clasped Eden in his warm arms and for a spell the troubled man ceased to argue with his unseen foe.

But seemed at peace for a time …

One lonely night found the travelers with no shelter but the land and sky, no dwellings nearby and no human flock to keep them company in a pasture of bare rocks. A night of stars but no moon and few clouds, so no rain fell to trouble them. The wind held its breath, and the warmth of their small campfire did not seem to fade until deep into the night.

The companions slept, heads curled on their arms, upon their folded robes. The lambs huddled together in a knot, and Eden dozed, pressed to her master's side. The last thing she remembered before sleep was the one called Judas looking at her across the campfire. He stared at her with bitter eyes. Dark eyes she couldn't meet. The troubled mind was upon Judas again, as though that terrible creature, the Hollow Man, sat upon his shoulder. The same as she knew before the cave, whispering poisoned words into Judas' ear. And as she laid her head down beside her master's thigh, she dreamt the strangest dream ...

Eden lay on a pallet of dank straw in a dark, damp garrison cell. A bar of light fell from a slit in a heavy door. Next to her, a sleeping prisoner breathed heavily—not her master, but the wild man of the river. He wore an iron collar about his neck fastened to the stone wall. Beyond the heavy door footsteps approached, echoing off an empty hall. The footsteps stopped outside the door. A key turned in a lock, and the hinges groaned.

A Roman Legionary stood in the hall, a stern soldier who held a sword.

"Baptist!" he ordered. "Get up."

In her dream Eden rose from her pallet, teeth bared, and leapt to the door. But her paws seemed stuck on the stone floor,

Eden

she couldn't pull them up, she couldn't move. There was just her will to move and the prison turnkey standing in the doorframe.

If only she could get to him, if only—

Samson's sudden bray woke Eden from her dream.

"The man of the river is *dead*," the donkey cried. "They've killed him."

Now the others were awake, startled by the noise. They sat up in alarm.

But who "they" were, Eden didn't know and the lambs began to bleat, "Who killed him? Who killed who?"

The companions huddled about the master. Eden looked wildly around, but there was no one near them in this bit of field. The road lay empty, nothing amiss. Judas went among the animals, quieting the sheep, then to Samson, petting his long ears. "The man of the river is dead," the donkey said sadly. "He who lifted my burdens, who set me free, who bid me walk with you … He is no more."

And Eden knew the donkey had dreamed the same dream.

She caught a curious look on the face of the one called Judas. The man had undergone a subtle change. He seemed to understand every bray that came out of Samson's mouth, and Eden wondered if he understood the language of animals now. Would he understand if she talked to him?

"Why do you look like that?" she growled.

And Judas gazed back at her with knowing eyes.

"I know you can understand me," Eden said. "Why don't you answer?"

But Judas merely smiled a crooked smile. The strangest feeling came over the dog that this was not the Judas they all knew, but someone or something else inside his skin. Was this the Hollow Man on the ledge looking at her? Was this the Adversary, then? Had that creature from the time in the wilderness somehow taken over Judas' sick and troubled mind?

The twisted hateful feelings slowly passed and after a moment Judas looked merely sad, and above all worried, troubled by his new powers ... as if understanding the words of beasts was unnatural and forbidden.

He let go of Samson's long ear, sat heavily in the midst of the lambs planting his hands upon his knees, and hung his head. The lambs crowded around him, hopeful as usual. "We're here! We're here!" they cried. And Eden came among them, forgiving him now his moment of weakness. She nosed his hand off his knee, nosed it and nosed it again, until he touched her head and stroked her white face.

"I'm all right," Judas told Eden. "Our master takes the pain away. And I return. But then I am still here. Alone with you."

Wind and Waves
✳ ✳ ✳

That day they marched without rest.

Dusk came, and as night fell the companions arrived again at the great lake. The travelers straggled like shipwreck survivors, strung out along the beach. Eden felt confused and lost. She walked along a sandbar as the ripples lapped quietly over her paws. Then she stood in the shallow tide pools with Samson the donkey, the lambs and the companions. A boat came to shore, and the companions pulled it close to the sandbar and climbed aboard. But their master stood aside, bidding them enter the boat, for he wished to be alone.

Judas lifted Eden over the gunwale into the others' waiting arms, and she wriggled in distress. But Judas calmed her, saying, "Come now, we'll be all right. Never so far he can't find us."

But as there was no room for the donkey in the boat, and no room for the lambs, they remained behind with their master. And once upon the sea Eden watched Samson standing on the shore, swishing his tail, while the cluster of lambs surrounded his legs and their master kneeled on the sandbar to pray.

As the boat sailed out to deeper water, the wind freshened and waves struck the bow; they slid into the swells and lost the land from sight. With each gust the swells mounted, causing the shore to vanish and reappear as they rode the slopes of a churning sea.

Back on the beach, Samson and the lambs retreated further and further from sight, yet even at a great distance Eden saw the other animals staring anxiously over the water while her master was nowhere to be seen. *Never so far?*

Dark clouds closed in from above and the wind sharpened. Now white-crested water splashed across their faces, raining into the belly of the boat.

And Eden became afraid.

The companions began to clamor in fear, clutching their oars and shouting into the wind as the sailcloth snapped above their heads. The mast shook and the sheets whipped away like writhing snakes.

The waves rose and dashed down. Everyone clung to a rope or plank to keep from being tossed over the side. Eden felt the gathering cry in every throat, a cry to heaven begging for their lives. The wind tried to shout them down but suddenly they did cry, Judas first among them. And he clasped Eden to his chest.

Their master stood upon the waves.

A few lengths from the tossing boat he beckoned them, as if to say, *if I can ... so can you....* Her master held out his hands to beckon her. Gently bobbing up and down, yet standing firmly in the trough, as one would stand in a field of wheat, the crests rising to his waist then falling to his calves. He stared boldly at the crowded boat, daring any of them to come to him. Any of them ...

One of the companions rose from his seat at the stern, leaving the tiller to another. Eden watched him as he prepared himself, slipping his robes from his shoulders and wrapping them around his waist, girding his loins. His face pale with fear, he put one leg over the gunwale, and then the other and stepped out of the boat. For a moment it seemed he would reach their master, for the waves and water did not swallow him up. He reached out like a baby learning to walk, took one step, then another—

And that's when the water, sensing his doubt, seized him. The surf took his limbs and he struggled in the sea like any other man.

Yet the fear and sickness left Eden and she struggled out of Judas' arms.

Once more, as with the drowning lamb in the river, she leapt from the boat. But a man was much bigger to save than a kid, and Eden floundered with the companion as the wind and waves tossed them about, from trough to crest and down again.

Was it a wave, or her master who brought them both back to the boat?

Not a wave. Though the companions' clothes were wet and dripping and Eden's white fur was soaked to the skin, her master remained for a moment. He rocked gently back and forth buoyed in the troughs, and then climbed into the boat with the rest. When he came aboard, his clothes were mostly dry, and with an easy hand he wiped away the spray from the waves that had beaded on his hair and face.

He held Eden close, so proud of her for being brave. She felt his mind full of praise as he petted her. Her master's safe arms seemed to glow through the damp wet, warming her spiky fur, deep into her body.

Now her master stared into the storm-wracked sky, challenging it to defy him. He glared boldly into the face of the waves and wind, even as his companions cowered in pale awe.

They had seen what they refused to accept, and yet still they could not deny their eyes.

Eden's master then sighed sadly in his heart of hearts, as though finally realizing what he could expect from those in the boat and what was too much to hope for.

Even the sky took notice.

The clouds shrank upon themselves and the wind calmed.

In a few moments the boat no longer rocked in the heavy troughs, and the sail luffed gladly. Judas clamped his arm about the till and grasped the sheet. The moon's face broke through the dark night, glistening over the water.

Samson the donkey and the lambs waited patiently on the shore as the boat sailed ever closer. The lambs clustered about Samson's legs, shuffling in anticipation. Eden leapt over the gunwale and shook all over.

The lambs bleated, "Did you walk *too*? Did youwalk?"

"No," Eden told them. "I paddled. I've always paddled."

"Ahem," Samson cleared his throat, getting ready for a pronouncement. He dipped his long gray nose, "Every little lamb should know by now it's best to paddle," he told them wisely.

And the lambs thought very seriously about this, softly bleating amongst themselves, "Paddle. Paddle. Best to paddle—"

Until Eden noticed her master's footprints in the sand and the companions hurrying to keep up. "Hush now!" she barked at the lambs.

Over the passing weeks Eden had grown accustomed to lambs that stayed young, that never grew up into sheep. And to old Samson who walked night and day without tiring. And more than delighted in her own strong limbs, for she ran all day long, dodging the old donkey as he stoically plodded forward, round and round the lambs, keeping everyone in line and on the move.

But other things began to change.

Changes the spry old dog couldn't quite put her paw on. For one thing, Eden seemed to hear everything human people kept inside their minds. Judas especially, of all the companions—Eden felt his every trouble. Pain from deep within twisted like a vine about a sapling, slowly strangling him. A deep ache turning his face into a mask of pain he could never take off. With every mile that passed he grew more and more fearful.

But something else had changed, something that troubled her, causing a kind of foreboding as they tramped toward each day's horizon. The light flickered in her master's eyes, a knowing look that spoke a thousand thoughts. The dog sensed their days together growing short, every moment precious. And Eden somehow knew their journey was drawing to a close.… Time like a candle burning to the nub.

Add to that, the stranger that came amongst them—

Not only to trouble Judas in his mind, but all of them, and in the flesh.

Eden remembered him well—their Adversary—the Hollow Man who'd tempted her master and herself in the wilderness. Long ago she knew the creature squatting before the empty cave could not be banished. Now she sensed him all around. Sometimes in the crowd listening at their master's feet. *There*, that man with the cowl over his head covering his face. Other times she sensed him hiding in a clump of trees, or sitting in a cluster of boulders at night. Eden sensed him every time he drew near, invisible like a breath of wind, a shadow on their heels even in the dark.

Whether close at hand or farther away, the Hollow Man almost always stayed within sight, and if not then within earshot … and if not, then trailing behind on the last turn in the road, with only a little swirl of dust for anyone to see.

Once Eden thought she caught him whispering in the ear of poor Judas, only to see her master's companion shrink away in horror. Judas stumbled toward her with his eyes covered as if he could not bear to behold this strange man. Then he clutched Eden desperately, his mind a black cloud of toil and confusion. She felt his tears upon her muzzle.

Samson noticed too, and perked his ears.

The lambs gathered around the strong donkey's legs as they often did when they felt him thinking, and this time he bid them, "Run away and play."

But the lambs only shuffled closer, and the animals watched over Judas for a long time. Until the man left off weeping and Eden could shake his tears from her nose.

The Women
✷ ✷ ✷

Then there were the women: one who begged them to save her, and the other who cursed Eden's master with all her might. Two women brought before them on the same day, both in a muddy street, beside the damp canvas stalls of merchants in a marketplace. The woman who begged them, they saved, and left her behind for she did not join them.

But the other who cursed with all her might stayed with them until the end.

That day the clouds rolled in over the sea and pelted their road with rain all morning. A troop of soldiers on horseback galloped past with the heavy thunder of hooves, kicking up wet dirt. Their faces splattered, their robes drenched, Samson the donkey a clopping mess, and Eden's silvery fur spiky where she'd run through puddled craters. Sodden lambs followed without complaint but none of them laughed. By the time Eden's master, the companions, Samson and the lambs entered the village they each wore the same coat of mud.

Stone houses passed on either side. The travelers felt a kind of dank anger clinging to the town, like dirty smoke hanging in the air. Before even finding some shelter—a merchant's stall or even the wet awning of an inn—the animals heard rumblings around the corner. The stone walls echoed with stamping feet and harsh voices.

An angry crowd burst out into the main way. An ugly mob: townsfolk, camel boys, wicked children and righteous hags, all shouting spittle-flecked oaths. They had chased a woman into the street. The hounded woman fell as she fled; then crawled through a puddle, wailing for anyone to help her.

Once again, Eden saw the Hollow Man standing close by.

Their Adversary lurked in the shelter of an arcade, then joined the crowd. Coming out from the overhang into the rain, he held out a handful of wet stones from the street, going from face to face, urging anyone who met his gaze to take them from his cupped hands. Flitting from person to person like a nagging fly, he spoke in this one's ear, gripped another's wrist, goading anyone who would listen, *"Look how she begs. Can't you tell she's guilty? She's guilty."*

The crowd reared up with a hundred clenched fists. They filled the street and rammed the stalls, jostling in all directions. The lambs were stepped on, bleating, and Samson turned his rear to kick—

Eden recoiled at the crowd, afraid of being trampled too.

The woman crawled on all fours to their master's feet and clutched the hem of his robe, her spirit broken. The rain pelted down and the woman's tears vanished on the wet paving stones.

Fear crept into Eden's limbs as the woman lay on the ground, too defeated to even plead for her life. But like that moment on the riverbank where Eden had seen the drowning lamb, the cluster of fear hardened to a knot of courage.

And suddenly there was no more thinking to be done—

Eden leapt in front to guard the woman's body.

And as the dog stood her ground the woman's scent filled

Eden's head. The smell of disgrace clung to her skin as though she lived among refuse, spoiled fish heads and moldy cloth—along with the stench of abandon, the stink of men waiting at her dwelling either in shame or lust or just because they knew she was there. For all travelers crossed her threshold, her doorway open to all comers.

Eden could see the place, a room of squalor, harsh perfume, stained curtains and threadbare pillows. A place where candle wax pooled on the tables, spilled wine on the floor and sweat filled the air. But that was just a scent that clung to a person, not her insides.

The woman herself did not smell of evil, just desperation and loneliness. Come to grovel and beg for her life. Eden did not clearly understand the woman's sin, but in her own way Eden understood why the crowd was angry. The woman had sinned against the pack and now the pack had turned on her.

Eden faced the mob. The dog bared her teeth, her fur bristled and she growled low.

"No closer! None of you!"

Eden spied their Adversary slyly grinning at her from behind two caravan slaves. *Oh, yes, he remembered her well.*

The first stone hit Eden as she stood over the broken woman, making her yelp. But she didn't run. The Hollow Man sneered, and picked up another stone. The woman cowered at their master's feet; she clasped his muddy ankles. Her frantic fingers picked at his worn sandal, as if the thin leather thongs might save her as she waited for the next blow. Any moment there'd be another stone, and then another, and then a dozen.

Eden growled again and stood her ground.

The mob's wrath caught in its throat. They held their stinking breath.

And no stone flew. Instead they shuffled back.

Because of a growling dog? Or because Eden's master refused to leave the woman's side, standing over them both? He reached down to the woman picking at his feet, took her hands from his sandals and then raised her up as she clutched his mud-splattered robe. He wiped the tears from her streaked face with the hem of her sleeve. But in total defeat, the woman sank to her knees, clutching a length of his cloak simply to steady herself.

A man in the front of the crowd raised a fist with a stone inside.

Eden could see their Adversary breathing words at the back of his head.

Yet something in her master's manner made the man pause. The rock weighed his hand down to his side. Eden pushed up against the woman, sheltering her. The dog could feel her body tremble. Their master stood his ground and reached into his purse. Searched for a moment and brought forth the two small stones: the black stone, white inside—and the white stone, its insides black.

He held the two small stones in his open palm; presenting them before the arc of ugly faces.

As if to say, *Take mine.*

As if to say, *Use them first on me.*

The mob held back, afraid to move. But the Hollow Man was not through prodding them. The clever creature kept whispering from ear to ear, the angry crowd reacting with every word. Eden could feel him too, his false smiles and doubting frowns, whatever served his purpose, offering false courage like bad wine. And soon the wretched faces began to laugh. To sneer. *What harm from two little pebbles? Let this muddy wanderer throw. Go ahead throw, Wise Man. There's nothing you can do to us.*

As if in answer her master gently cast the two stones upon the muddy street.

The two stones rolled beside a brown puddle. Rubbed together for so long you could plainly see the black inside the white stone and the white inside the black.

Pick up mine, he seemed to say.

Use my two stones.

But no one moved to take them.

The false courage in this pack of humans began to wither.

"Go on!" the Hollow Man hissed from deep within the crowd. "What are you waiting for?"

Eden's master stood his ground.

The rain began to lighten as rivulets ran down the house fronts like weeping tears, down stone drains, flowing away to nothing. The clouds tore themselves to shreds above their heads and many hands began to tremble. Each man or woman feeling their sins upon themselves, dousing their anger, as the clouds rent ragged slashes in an open sky. And her master stood his ground staring at the cowed faces. As if to say—

He who is without sin …

As if to say—

Cast the first stone.

Did he actually speak out loud? Or did Eden hear it only in her mind?

He must have spoken.

For no one in the crowd moved or said a word. Or threw a stone.

The mob's anger dissolved like salt in water, leaving nothing but a bitter taste. In a few moments Eden lost sight of the Hollow Man. Their Adversary seemed to give up and fade into the bowels of the crowd. And in another few moments the crowd itself began to break apart, for nothing really held this pack together except hate for this poor woman who had breached their laws. All the life had gone out of each and every ugly face, and with it, their common purpose. Soon the street stood empty. When Eden looked for Samson and the lambs, she saw they had retreated from the crowd, standing in a knot with the companions.

Leaving only Eden.

Her master.

And the woman at his feet.

Eden licked the woman's face and tasted the common mud of every common town. The woman smiled back at Eden with all her heart—

A cup of thanks, filled to overflowing.

The woman no longer smelled of sin, or the stink of strangers or harsh perfume. Her endless downfall had been gently broken by the offer of two stones, now lying by a muddy puddle. Two stones rubbed together for so long you could plainly see the black inside the white stone and the white inside the black.

Now like every other pebble in the street.

The companions prepared to leave this ugly town. All of them felt dirtier than the muddy road or the dung splattered on their wet clothes. But their master would not leave. This town was no worse than a dozen others they'd visited. Instead he bid them find shelter under the brick arcade till the weather cleared, for it had begun to rain again. Eden scrambled underneath the overhang with the others, as did the lambs, who wandered up and down the empty arcade shaking their wet fleece. But there was no room for Samson who stood forlornly in the street as raindrops dripped from his drooping ears.

"Well, there's enough room for you under there," he complained to Eden. "But they gave away my blanket to a donkey in the last village!"

"I'd give you my coat, but I can't," Eden told him. "It's attached."

"Oh stop," Samson replied. "If we hadn't saved the woman we'd have been on our way to somewhere better."

"Would it help if I came out and sat in the rain with you?" Eden asked.

Samson thought for a moment. "No, send out some of the lambs. They keep my legs warm."

But none of the lambs were handy. Curious and restless as ever, they had wandered to the far end of the overhang and discovered they were not alone. "Oh look!" they exclaimed. "We found a person. A person! What is your name, Person?"

A pitiful creature crouching in the shadow of the wall looked at them with dangerous eyes. Yet another woman, rags clinging to her, legs and hands and face smeared with dirt, her hair a wild nest about her head. The lambs shook their tails to show they were friendly and crowded in close bleating, "Hello, Person. Hello, Person!"

But the ragged woman scuttled back against the wall and snarled, hands outstretched. Fingers like claws.

The lambs broke in every direction, crying:

"Oh my! Oh my!"

Samson plodded purposefully over to see what the fuss was all about.

"She's mad," the donkey told his lambs. And they looked

at him with puzzlement on their velvet muzzles. Eden trotted back and forth to herd the lambs off.

"Come away from here," she warned. "You might get bit."

The woman now crouched by some bits of broken stone, waving invisible flies from her face, cursing at them with words Eden didn't understand. She reminded Eden of Judas when he talked to himself. Yet Eden knew that this one, this woman, never talked to anyone *but* herself.

The rain had stopped once more and the travelers gathered their slim goods together in preparation for another march. With a deep sigh, Samson turned to go. Perhaps this town *was* better than the empty road. Eden nudged the lambs and they followed in the donkey's hoof steps. Then the companions, last of all, abandoned the town without a second thought, trudging out from the brick arcade and leaving the woman to her voices. Eden's sharp ears heard the poor creature scuttle off, withdrawing to the dark safety of her stony wall, still muttering to herself.

But they had not seen the last of her.

They walked till sunset, and in the growing dusk Eden heard the sound of soft footsteps along the side of the road. Ah, the fox had returned, the wary fox following them as quietly as possible. Eden had sensed him dogging their trail on and off since the start of their great journey. With each sign and marvel, with each wonder she sensed him near enough to see or catch a scent yet reluctant to show himself.

She considered asking him to join them again. But after a moment thought *no*; his stealthy footsteps showed that however curious he might be, the fox wanted to keep things as they were. To see and not be seen, and no animal would fault another for that.

The travelers stopped among a cluster of damp boulders.

So, they would sleep outside tonight. Or, not so much sleep as dozing in fits and starts. No dry wood for a fire; a long, cold camp, nodding in the clammy dark.

More worrisome still, as nightfall's last gray curtain fell Eden saw Judas sneak off alone. The unhappy man stood for some moments in the black shadow of a stunted tree. At first it appeared Judas was speaking into the air as he'd often done before. But then Eden smelled the fox again lying low in a scrap of brush. The fox's ears stood up, quivering as he listened. Yes, listened patiently … creeping closer and closer until he crouched only a step away from the man's feet. Much too close for comfort. But stranger still, Judas knew the fox was close, close enough to overhear him. For suddenly Judas spoke to the fox just as he had learned to do with all the other animals, seeing into their minds and listening to their thoughts.

"I'm afraid," the man told him. And the fox cocked his ears. "I have doubts," Judas said.

The fox sniffed his paw, then licked some sand from between his pads.

"This can't be right, can it? Am I really this alone? Does no one else doubt?"

But the fox made no reply. And then the man knew the fox would not answer him. Sadly, Judas crept back to the group before anyone was aware of his absence.

He sought out Eden in the cluster of rocks.

And when he snuggled against her fur she felt that his hands were cold.

Eden awoke to the sound of heavy breathing in the cluster of rocks.

Another visitor had joined them in the night.

Her eyes hadn't snapped open to footsteps in the dark, but to the sound of the newcomer muttering indistinct words. Eden recognized the voice: the madwoman huddled in the stone arcade. She was close, only a few paces off, mumbling under her breath. Yet near enough for Eden to hear her muffled words. Many voices argued in her head.

You know him.

I know him too.

No, you don't.
Yes, yes, I do.

The crazy woman must have kept out of sight along the way, approaching ever closer in the dark. Eden sensed nothing evil in this creature, only like Judas, the woman was wracked by confusion and sadness and fear. And Judas seemed to recognize her as well, muttering, "Ah, the woman who talks to flies."

None of their master's companions rose to greet her in the dark.

But no one chased her away either.

Those things were best left till morning, when the rule of night receded and you could see by daylight. These days strangers often approached from orchard, path or field. In recent months the travelers had often woken to visitors in their midst, a newcomer appearing to talk or listen, so one more body was of no account.

But the animals felt differently about this woman, and all night they were aware of her presence. The man named Judas might argue with himself, but he always returned from that dark, solitary talking room. The woman who talked to flies disturbed them more, arguing on and on, for she dwelt in a place of no return.

So the animals held a meeting of their own as dawn approached. They gathered head to head to share their thoughts. As usual the lambs talked over each other, crowding around Samson's long gray nose.

Softly bleating, "Why is she talking? Why won't she stop? Will she herd us? Will she shear us? Will she *bite* us?"

Until the donkey sternly brayed for quiet.

"One voice with so many tongues makes no sense whatsoever!" he scolded.

This confused the poor lambs even more and they hung their heads, glancing at Eden to see what she thought.

"I think the lambs are right," Eden said, and Samson snorted in surprise. "This woman is both scary and not scary at the same time," the dog told them.

Samson wrinkled his forehead and twitched his ears thinking hard.

"Let the lambs who are not afraid go to comfort her," Eden said, "and let the lambs who are afraid stay with us."

"And what shall you and I do?" Samson finally asked.

"We shall do what we always do," the dog told him. "You and I shall guard the lambs—whether they are afraid or not."

Samson considered this for many long moments. He had never considered himself a guard of anyone. Always a beast of burden—to fetch and carry, to be driven, whipped and never complain. But now he realized he was more than merely a freed slave. He was his own donkey, for better or worse.

"You are a very wise dog," he said at last to Eden.

"Then let the lambs do as they do, and we shall do as we do."

The lambs heard her clearly and they approached the madwoman with caution, the boldest at the front, the shyest behind. One lamb, two lambs, three lambs, four … soon they surrounded her. The woman of the invisible flies swatted the air about her head, ruffling her hair for invisible gnats, and kept swatting until the rising sun finally struck her face. The morning light slanted across the boulders and the stunted trees. Dawn had come, the light and warmth driving the night chill away.

Their master made his way through the cluster of lambs and looked down. Sunlight sat on his shoulder. The woman shielded her face, and swatted more flies that did not exist.

Eden nosed her way through the clinging lambs till she reached her master's legs, getting close enough to see.

The woman held out a clenched fist, then turned palm up and opened her fingers.

Two stones rested inside her hand; the black stone with the white inside and the white stone with the black. In returning the two worn stones, she offered the only gift she had. Of course, she had overheard their master's words in the muddy street back in the ugly town. *Who was she to cast away these two precious stones?*

If the two stones their master had taken from his purse had saved a condemned woman from a vengeful crowd ... might they not save her as well? By returning the black stone and the white, might she not exchange them for a touch of sanity? Sanity for two smooth rocks? Anything to quiet the many voices in her head.

"Can I travel in your purse too?" the woman of invisible flies asked.

"All are welcome to come with me."

Their master smiled at the two stones in her palm. "I was afraid I had lost those for good." He then took her hand in his and folded her fingers closed, the stones inside.

"But why don't you hold them for a while? Perhaps if we travel together we'll come to know each other, and like those stones that traveled in my purse so long, you too can show your insides without breaking."

Their master gently lifted the woman's chin.

Looking at her as if to say, *Know me ...*

For several moments the woman went through many changes, speaking words but not to flies this time. Saying the same words in different order and every time a different way—

First bitterly, "*You* ..."

Then after a moment, with a question; as if to ask, *have we met before?*

"*Do* I know you ...?"

Then softening, "Yes. I think I know you."

Becoming surer in her thought, "Yes I *know* I know you."

For a moment, her eyes darted about to a fly that really wasn't there, then down at her clenched fist. The stones lay in her hand, safe and sound. Looking at their master's face once more, accepting what she finally knew for certain.

"Yes. I know you."

Come Forth
✸ ✸ ✸

A great wind came out of the east with the rising sun.
    The clouds overhead slashed across a blue sky.
And the wind dried the fallen rain off the skin of the land.
That day's march promised to be as cold as the night before. The travelers clutched their robes about them, and those in tatters clutched their rags, waiting for someone to take the first step. It seemed much simpler to stand shivering than make the effort to move.

As they milled about Eden noticed the most curious thing. How this woman who once saw invisible flies came upon them so quietly in the night. Why they never heard her footfalls until she fell upon them.

Her feet were bare.

No sandals, not even cloth bindings. Her toes blue from cold, her heels red with cuts. Eden crept close, unsure if she was welcome, but the woman made no sudden movement. Eden sniffed her pale feet very thoughtfully, learning everything there was to know about them. The woman had been walking on bare feet and thick calluses for a long time. And Eden could smell the soot of solitude, the dust of a thousand roads and a thousand empty streets. A thousand barred doors against a woman who wandered alone and who talked to invisible flies.

Yet of the wounds themselves, some were new, the cuts fresh; others old and draining. And Eden smelled the ominous taint, the beginning of infection. The woman's bruised feet could go either way, heal or rot ...

Eden's smart nose drew ever closer, sniffing round and round. What was to be done? *What could be done?* Eden knew only one thing to do: lick the cut and make it better. Licking always helped. *See here now, Cut. I will fix you, Cut, lick and lick until you're better. Licking always helps you heal. Pay attention, Cut.*

Eden went at the woman's foot, sniffing and licking round and round, making sure no part was missed. And the woman giggled as the dog's breath tickled her toes and Eden's warm tongue soothed the cuts. But the woman who once talked to flies wouldn't let her keep licking forever. She petted Eden's head and whispered:

"No, no little one. You needn't do that. I'll be fine. I'll be fine."

The companions stood about with twisted mouths and covetous eyes, that their dog should be so kind to a stranger, when they themselves felt so little for the woman. Judas stared hardest of all, and Eden read his mind, *you never loved me that way ...*

But instead of hurrying them off on the day's march, their master only chuckled to himself, gathered his robes under him, and sat on a nearby boulder. Then suddenly he laughed out loud, needing only to touch the thong of one sandal to break the spell that held the companions in thrall. They saw their master tugging at his ankles and rushed to offer the woman the sandals off their own feet:

"Here, Maryam, take mine. No, take mine! Here, Maryam, take mine!"

But it was Judas who owned the moment. He tugged on the drawstring of his shoulder sack and produced a pair of brand-new sandals. Eden could even smell the fresh oil on the leather.

"Take mine, Maryam," Judas said quietly. "I have extra."

The madwoman, who once talked to flies, looked up at the sound of her name from face to face. She held Eden's head in her hands, stroking her ears. She looked down at her naked feet, naked for how long? She couldn't remember. How many years had it been since she had worn anything on her feet? She didn't know.

"Can you help me tie them?" Maryam asked of Judas. "My fingers have forgotten."

Eden watched Judas help the woman, putting on one sandal and then the next. "Maryam," Judas said to her, part in pity and part disdain. "A common enough name."

"And my mother's ..." their master said quietly.

Eden knew what her master meant. For neither the woman who once talked to flies nor the carpenter's woman were in any way common. And Eden realized there were things about people she would never understand. So cruel and yet kind, so brave and yet scared. But perhaps most confusing of all, that people never sought beneath the surface, to know your deepest scent.

Yet the woman who spoke to flies had sought them out despite her fear, sought them out on bare feet with nothing between her and the cold, hard ground. Sought them out to return two stones, the black stone with the white inside and the white stone, black within ...

Eden smelled the woman's feet inside her new sandals, then sniffed and licked a little more. The cuts were already draining, the woman's feet healing. Eden went back again for

good measure, each gentle touch of her tongue making the wounds better and better:
See now, Cut, I cleaned you.
See now, Cut, I closed you.
See now, Cut, I fixed you.

Suddenly the wind paused for a moment and a quiet urgency swept over the travelers. Their master looked to the horizon as though hearing a silent call. And suddenly he rose from his boulder and strode out alone, taking even Eden by surprise. While the rest—Samson, the lambs, the companions and the newcomer, Maryam in her new sandals—all rushed to keep up.

The group struck out at a great pace along the road, but with every step forward the gales of wind pressed against them, snatching their robes and tugging their limbs. The gusts pushed back almost as strongly as they struggled forward. And despite how hard they slogged, one foot in front of the other, the landscape slowly ground to a halt beneath their feet.

A great force, a great will wanted them moving and on the march. But within the wind a fierce defiance, like a wall, held them back. A divine will urged them to stumble on, but denied them passage. The earth seemed to refuse to yield. A force prodded them on, yet a stubborn hand prevented them from gaining ground, reaching the next rise, the next orchard, the next field. It seemed as though all of them—man, woman, animal—were destined to stagger forward only a step at a time with nothing to show for all their effort.

The wind ripped across Eden's nose, whistling in her ears. She felt her legs struggling, the old weakness again, dragging her down. The dog looked at Samson, whose eyes said, *How can I be so tired?...* And the lambs of course, suddenly and for the very first time complaining all at once, "The wind is so great. The ground is so hard! The pebbles so sharp! *Our feet! Oh, our poor feet!*"

Yet even as they walked and struggled on, Eden could feel her master's will growing with every step. Weary though they were, no force on earth could stop him going on.

Where were they going? No one knew.

Yet all feared they would arrive too late.

The tempest swirled about them and yet they trudged on, one foot in front of the next. Eden watched the sun rise in the east, pass overhead and set in the west. And still they marched on through the night. The sun rose, the sun set, another day, another night—yet still the travelers never paused to rest. Walking in place to *nowhere*, trapped between where they were going and where they had been. Caught between what lay ahead and what fell behind, an endless road that never changed.

At last, after what seemed leagues and leagues, the wind buffeted them to a halt and they pulled up short where they stood, stumbling upon one another. A confused knot of people and animals milled about at the edge of a lonely pasture. They had stopped in silent agreement, too weary to push on yet too weak to go back. Like strangers lost in a foreign land, not knowing where to turn.

The wind sighed as if pleased with all their effort, and on its wings floated a soft voice. Someone or something was calling out to them. In that moment they saw a servant girl running down the road, her head bare, waving a headscarf in her hand. Crying and begging, clearly desperate, but the wind swallowed her words.

She seemed to know them; halting a hundred paces off, she waved the scarf frantically for everyone to see. *Come on! Come on!* she begged. *Come with me!*

And all who saw her overcame their weariness, their invisible shackles cast away, free to run, free to follow her. The servant girl led them over the crest of a hill, down a slope and then up another hill. And suddenly it struck Eden that this part of the country seemed familiar. They'd been here before. But where had they *not* gone? Over the course of the year they had walked over their own footsteps a dozen times.

The servant girl paused on the next crest. Below them lay a well-tended field and a large white stone house behind a high stone wall. Something seemed familiar about the place. Then Eden remembered ... they had tarried here for water and a short rest, months and months ago. The servant girl was leading them to the fine house and rich orchard of a very pious man and his sisters. But the companions had not returned in all this time.

As the servant girl reached the courtyard walls, the household poured from the doors to meet the travelers, and many strangers were among them. People from nearby homes and farms had been waiting inside the enclosure, wailing and in grief, for the lord of these fields and orchards, the Pious Man of this house, had died.

Eden, Samson and the lambs stopped short of joining the crowd, hesitant to mingle with those so clearly distressed. A momentary fear ran through the animals, that mourners in such great pain might do something rash. Strangely at this moment, Eden could no longer understand the minds or words of people, as though the wind had swept that power from her. She looked to Samson to see if he understood, but he only hung his head and dipped his ears as if ashamed. And when she caught the donkey's eye she saw he understood as little as she.

The lambs hid behind them both; the single thought racing through the flock: *weddings and funerals, very bad for lambs.* There were always fewer lambs after such ceremonies. Perhaps not knowing every word that passed between people made for purer hearts, like a cloak of silence shielding the animals from ugliness. But in any case, the animals saw what they saw even if the power to read minds had abandoned them, and what they saw was not pleasing to their eyes.

Among those who poured through the house gates was an angry Rabbi with a very sour face and one of the devout man's sisters, clutching her headdress close about her face. Eden could not hear what the woman said, as she hissed in the Rabbi's ear, but the grieving sister was clearly angry at their master. Suddenly the grieving sister left the Rabbi's side and accosted their master, cutting off any reply. The sister wrung her hands in grief, her eyes accusing, demanding, *why didn't you come whilst my brother was sick? Why?*

The Rabbi nodded sternly at every word she spoke, while frowning at the travelers with a mouth that bled contempt. Everyone could tell what the sister was thinking. If their master had wanted to see his beloved friend, *why not come earlier? There was time enough.* But look now, *too late! Too late!*

Their master suffered the sister's harsh tongue without objection.

Then Judas came forward and tried to explain that they had all been delayed on the road, but the sour Rabbi glared him into silence. Judas shrank away, returning to the lamb's fold. Eden and Samson heard him whisper to the lambs, "Her brother is dead. We came too late."

But the sister, still resentful, pointed into the house where the other sister remained hidden, and pointed to the great crowd of mourners, all gathered to pay their respects.

And Judas muttered under his breath, glancing at the lambs, "If there is to be a funeral feast, things will not go well for you."

The lambs began to shuffle nervously, wondering whether to flee, whether to flee *right now*. But no one tried to herd them into the enclosure, and the crowd grew suddenly hushed, taking a step back.

The second sister appeared in the doorway of their house as if in a trance. She recognized no one, but then paused for a moment beside Eden's master. And though their master tried to comfort the second sister with soft words, she did not seem to hear. The first sister still harangued all nearby, with a voice like rusty nails.

After a moment, the dazed sister left the doorway and slowly walked across the enclosure and onto the road. Her headscarf fell to her shoulder but she let it go, and all saw quite clearly where she went—to the rocky hill and the cave of the grave itself.

Eden's master bowed his head and followed. The animals feared to stay with the crowd and trotted after him, followed by Judas and the companions. All of them suddenly felt greater fear than any could remember, for the people dogged their heels and some among them spoke cold and bitter words.

The Rabbi pushed his way to the front of the crowd, seeking to lead them. Yes, he had been to the grave when the Pious Man had died and wanted all to know. A narrow cave, a slab covering the rock mouth, and nothing to see. Just dead Lazarus, and if you didn't believe him, come look for yourself.

When they reached the tomb the crowd stood about and

the words got even uglier. Yet Eden saw that some among them looked upon her master with pity in their eyes. He groaned as he approached the blank slab of stone, as though simply to look at the face of stone filled him with weakness and pain.

Sorrow fell from her master as he discarded his cloak. He covered his face with naked hands and wept. And Eden could feel why: for the loss of this man, for being too late, for staying in one place while the wind brought time to a standstill. Eden came to him so he knew she was there. As he wept, salty tears slipped through her master's hands and fell upon her nose. Without thinking she licked them off her nose. They tasted of water and life.

At this the trance seemed to fall from the silent sister, and she stared hard at the rock slab of the tomb as though to pierce it with her eyes. She placed her hands upon the slab, and then her forehead. She knew what lay behind, dead brother, Lazarus, four days gone. Dead all the while the travelers had been on the road to nowhere.

Eden could smell it too, the scent of dead flesh that crept from the tomb. Decay. The rank odor of *nevermore*. Suddenly the dog was aware the Hollow Man had joined them. The creature from the wasteland had slithered out of thin air, and stood innocently among the onlookers. He first approached the companions and tried to speak to Maryam of the invisible flies, and then to Judas, but they shunned him. So instead, the Hollow Man went to the Rabbi's ear and whispered for some time.

But the Rabbi turned his head to listen when Eden's master finally spoke, his voice so low all strained to hear him. And though Eden could barely hear her master's words, they struck her heart, and she understood these were the words her master whispered to the silent sister in the doorway of the house.

Words which came into her head on the faintest heartbeat, the faintest breath of thought, *I am the resurrection, and the life: he that believeth in me, though he were dead, yet shall he live: And whosoever liveth and believeth in me shall never die* ...

The distant sister, no longer in a trance, looked sharply at their master, hearing his words as though for the first time. And Eden heard something even stranger—the sound of movement beyond the stone slab. She went to the wall of rock and listened closer, yes, something inside the tomb was moving. Eden scratched at the tomb, whined and scratched again, *if only she could speak, if only*—

Then the distant sister shrieked, for she heard something beyond the stone as well. Many hands rushed to the slab and pushed and pulled and finally rolled away the stone from the place of the dead.

Eden heard her master's voice rise strongly, boldly to heaven for all to hear. It rang off the rocks, off every upturned face and echoed in every ear.

"Lazarus!" he cried. *"Lazarus, come forth."*

And out of the dark mouth of the cave the figure of the Pious Man appeared. Both sisters, the wailing and the silent one, clasped each other. Pale and faint, they swooned and many hands rushed to catch them. Then more hands came to remove their brother's shroud. For the man, once dead, now stood among them.

The Rabbi with the mouth of contempt held his head in awe, his face whiter than a winding cloth. Other mourners helped him find a place where he could sit without falling over. Whether he was stunned, blinded by a stroke of light or smitten at this wondrous sight Eden could not tell. But when the dog looked from mourner to mourner the Hollow Man was nowhere to be seen.

As for her master, his face had turned ashen, the blood drained away. And like the Rabbi he sought a safe seat on which to rest. Even as he sank exhausted into the arms of Judas and Maryam, he raised his eyes to heaven. Eden couldn't catch his words, but in her mind she heard and felt her master's everlasting thanks to God for answering his prayer. Words to the divine Almighty, mumbling words of thanks:

You heard.

Palm Fronds
✳ ✳ ✳

The travelers knew where they were going now.
Their feet took them up from rugged lands and dusty footpaths to broad roads paved with stone. The travelers passed orchards in early bud and simple villages on the edges of nowhere, always heading to the same place: the gates of the great city. So many witnessed their passing that word spread far and wide, and a great clamor rose that their master would come within the city walls again, this time to the temple feast.

Eden padded alongside Samson the donkey, and with every step the hard road told the dog its secrets. Endless traffic and throngs of callused feet had worn the paving stones and stained them. The stains were like dried tears beneath her paws, the ghosts of ancient troubles, whispers of the past.

Thirty years gone. Thirty years and more …

Long ago, two dogs and a donkey had traveled this very road fleeing the soldiers of a king. The dogs were Eden's ancestors, guarding father and mother and infant child in their flight, and a donkey much like Samson carrying ducks and pups and carpenter's tools down to the land of the great river. Then after years of exile on the riverbank, eating many fish and mending the carts among countless camel trains, the travelers returned over this same highway heading north, a lone caravan, unmarked by prying eyes.

And just as now, a road studded with crosses where dead men hung in silence.

As Eden, Samson and the lambs drew closer to the great city, so too the scores of hanging men rose to greet them, not with words, but with dead eyes and crows for company. Overhead, the sun rose to noon. The shadows below the timbers shrank to nothing while rats gathered to worship at the base of the crosses. Wild dogs without names came to eat the rats. And the lambs became afraid.

"Don't look," Eden told them. "Stay close, little ones and nothing will happen to you." But the lambs were not comforted and in the silence of fear hastened forward, eyes downcast, not daring to be left behind. Some ways off Eden heard the fox padding craftily along in and out of bushes and rocks, not letting himself be seen, but muttering to himself, "Rats but no cats, busy, busy, busy ..."

League after league these terrible sights mounted, but the travelers pressed on, taking deep breaths and long strides. Eden's master first, leading them closer and closer to the walls of the city, for he neither shrank nor quailed at the sight of dead men. As word spread of their approach the mice of the field gathered in multitudes, waving spears of grass as they had once before in Galilee, crying, "Behold! Behold! So glad you're here, so glad you've come!"

Then those who had heard rumors of gaudy marvels and vulgar magic shows crowded the travelers before the city gates hoping for a spectacle. Human feet rushed in, driving the joyful mice back to their holes, pressing the travelers from every side.

"Back! Back!" Samson brayed.

But no one listened.

"Back! Back!" Eden growled.

A few people shuffled back, but even greater throngs drove closer, so eager to see the man so many had heard so much about. And suddenly the lambs bleated in fear, bumping into one another as clumsy feet trampled their tiny hooves. Rough hands pushed the lambs aside, shoving the poor creatures about and it was everything the companions could do just to keep from being overwhelmed.

Judas and Maryam tried to bring some order to the mob, thrusting their hands against the jostling bodies, shouting at people who wouldn't listen, but finally stumbling back in defeat, knocking into Samson and stepping on Eden's tail.

The dog yelped and Judas cried:

"I'm sorry, I'm sorry, but they're mad. Mad!"

Maryam thrust her hand up to Judas' face and showed him the two stones, the black and the white. Despite the chaos she gently touched his robe.

"No, they only came to see. They mean no harm."

Judas jerked his arm away as if it burned.

"How would *you* know?" he said to Maryam. "You talked to *flies*."

Yet even as the man and woman tried to shelter the frightened animals, others came to rescue them. Others from nearby, who carefully threaded their way through the crowd. Unlike the grasping ones, these came to pour oil on the waters. Seeing the travelers and animals beset on every side, they drew calm out of chaos. Others who knew of these strange travelers, who had heard of them for many months—not as charlatans but as companions to a great healer who comforted the sick, who taught any who would listen.

And it suddenly struck Eden that the ugly crowd surrounding

them was like the white stone with black inside, and the kinder ones that appeared out of nowhere were like the black stone with the white.

These others advanced waving long palm fronds, just like the mice, placing them on the ground before the feet of the travelers to prepare the way. And upon seeing this, many of the ugliest in the crowd—the thrill seekers, the pickpockets, the drunks and the idly curious—left off their grasping allowing the lambs and the companions a moment's peace. Stepping back, the ugly ones allowed the pious ones with the palms to take their place.

The lambs gathered by Samson and Eden were petted and fawned upon, for no one in this new crowd wanted to see the animals hurt or taken. These were the ones who sought out Eden's master, not to clutch at his magic robe, but to stand in his presence and near any who followed him. To catch a sacred word, if by chance it fell.

Judas called for many hands, saying, "He shall not walk. Let not his feet touch the ground!" And the companions helped their master onto the donkey's back.

Eden worried for Samson; he had not carried any weight for many months. "Are you going to be all right?" she asked. And the donkey nodded.

"He is no burden," Samson said to Eden. "A year of walking has made me strong, and made him light as a bundle of flowers."

More palm fronds were laid at the travelers' feet, a green carpet through the gates and into the city. As Eden stepped on each green leaf her agile paws felt the tree from which the palm had been cut.... Palm trees that grew along the seashore by fishermen's nets, and date palms from orchards where sweet dates grew. There were palms from oases where camel caravans watered, and palms from hovels outside the city walls.

Yet some fronds came from palms along roads Roman Legionaries traveled, and these fronds told a darker tale. Trees cut down for the condemned, men worth less trouble than other men. For not all the condemned merited crosses and crossbeams. Common criminals, unlucky debtors, rebellious slaves and many more found a simpler end, hanging from a single post or nailed to a roadside trunk beside a rocky stream.

And over these fronds Eden tread carefully. The names of the hanging men cried out to her, I was Lucius, a galley sailor, *I struck my captain.* I was Aaron, *wife-murderer.* I was Gideon, son of Jacob, *orphan and goat thief.* Names upon names, all hung on stakes, all crucified, all dead.

As the city walls towered before them, Eden saw the fox peeking out from a drain hole. The fox met the dog's eyes, and she could read his mind. *No I'm not following you in there. A city is no place for a fox. No city streets for me.* The fox eyed the many rats scuttling along the city walls and licked his chops, but dared not pounce, not in daytime and not with crowds about.

Several rats in the shadow of the walls paused their running to watch the travelers pass. And one muttered to another:

"So this is who we're supposed to follow. Hurry and tell the others to keep an eye on him. Hurry and tell …"

The last thing Eden saw as she passed through the city gate was the Hollow Man. The low creature had joined their procession and waved a palm frond like the others, before placing it upon the paving stones with all the rest. And the rat who muttered *Hurry hurry* picked up that exact palm stem in his mouth and scurried off into its hole.

By What Authority
✳ ✳ ✳

Such commotion echoed through the city! Eden heard her master's name proclaimed over and over, and on every tongue. So even as the travelers came once again to the great temple, the merchants and herdsmen and money changers were not taken by surprise this time. They knew of his approach and remembered his wrath.

Before the travelers could even rest their burdens on the temple wall, word spread over the walls and through the compound, and all those inside rushed to pack up their goods and fold their tables. Instead of waiting for the travelers to enter, instead of waiting for Eden's master to chastise them again for trespass in the sacred precinct, they packed their coins and weights and measures, they rushed to drive their animals through the gate, while others opened their birdcages, letting their doves and pigeons and sparrows fly into the sky, singing, free.

Eden and Samson stood under the temple wall by the great doors. Eden's master dismounted from Samson's back. But instead of breathing relief, the donkey sighed as though the weight of the world had fallen once more on his shoulders. "I feel heavier unburdened than when I carry him," he told Eden. "Why is that?"

Eden could only wonder, but she knew there was nowhere she would rather be than in their master's presence.

"I don't know," she told the donkey. "But standing in his shadow I am never cold." Her master glanced at them as if he heard the animals speaking, then bid them follow him. He pushed past the tall, purple curtains and through the temple gates.

Many inside the compound bowed as the travelers entered. But a group of men by the stone altar *did not* bow, for they were not of the priestly cast, nor the merchant class nor the rabble, and so had nothing to fear of their master. Instead they invited the travelers to sit among them, including the dog, the donkey and the lambs, for these creatures were neither the first nor the last animals to wander inside the sacred walls.

Unlike the simple country folk who welcomed the companions on their travels, these were not simple men but the learned of the temple. Eden could see in their faces their thoughts were not about the fields' seasons or the day's catch from the sea, or even earthly power, but to seek truth in the power of thoughts, wishing only to pose questions and ponder answers. For the Learned Ones wondered if this man and his companions might know more of the mind of God than they, as so much lay hidden from them. And Eden heard their questions as easily as if she'd been one of them herself, knowing their thoughts and knowing their minds.

"Who gave you the truth you tell us? Who set you on this path?" The questions came one after another. "Did he speak in words? Or have you always known? We have many priests and rabbis. By what authority are you doing all these things?" And Eden watched her master listen carefully. He pointed at Samson standing silently in the midst of the lambs.

"Behold," their master said. "There is John of the River's beast of burden. Know you how he came to be John the Baptist's animal?"

The holy men did not know what to say. But Eden saw they were not satisfied with this reply. What difference did it make how the wild man of the river came by his beast? So her master persevered.

"I will answer your question if you answer mine. I will tell you who gave me the truth, who set me on this path, whether he spoke words or whether I have always known *if you can tell me* of John's blessing in the waters. Where did *his* anointing come from? Was it from heaven or from earth? Human or divine? Was his blessing from this donkey, or from God?" And now the learned men of the temple huddled together to ponder an answer.

Eden stood apart for a moment; she smelled something familiar, something out of the past. The feeling of fear, fear without words.

Then she saw where it came from: a bed of straw by the stone altar. One last lamb had been tied to an iron ring, unable to break away. The tiny lamb stared at the free animals in wonder. How could anyone else in the world be free when she was still tied down? How could anyone else in the world live without an iron collar about their neck? The lamb at the altar steps looked from her fellow lambs without iron rings about their necks, then to the gray donkey and at the white dog. Saying what all lambs said when tethered to the chain:

"This morning I was in a pen with my herd," she said. "But now I'm here. They say they sold me for my beautiful fleece, but I don't believe anyone told me the truth. Have you come to free me?" the tiny lamb asked.

Eden did not know how to reply. The companions weren't here for this one.

The dog looked to the wise old donkey, but Samson only wagged his head. He didn't know either. No one knew what to say. And the free lambs mingled about, asking each other in whispers, "Have we come to free her? Do we know the truth? I don't. Do you? I don't. Do you?"

Then Judas, who understood the language of beasts, came forward with Maryam, the woman who once talked to flies. Both struggled with the young lamb's collar seeking to free her, yet even as they tugged and plucked, the iron collar refused to open. Frustrated, the two kept jangling the chain, prying at the iron band, all to no avail. The collar refused to budge and the lamb bleated, her neck growing raw.

Still the learned men muttered among themselves, ignoring everything else, clearly confused. And Eden knew why, for there was no simple answer as to whether the wild man of the river had been blessed by the Almighty or not.

Eden with her sharp ears could hear them arguing among themselves.

"If we say God anointed John of the River, then we must answer why did we not follow him or go to the river to be anointed like the others? We must answer for this. Why did we not go like the others who came to take his blessing and saw him and knelt as water touched their heads? But if we say the blessing was human-made, then we might as well say the blessing came from that jackass that John owned. If we say human-made, then all those who knelt before John will be angry with us, and we will be stoned in the streets, for John is their prophet. He who prophesized the coming of the One, this very one who stands before us now ..."

At length none of the learned men could settle on what to say. Like the lamb chained to the altar by an iron collar, they had no answer and could not break free. So the lead rabbi among them simply said, "No, we don't know whether the man's words were human or divine, whether his anointing came from God or man or beast. No, none of us can say."

And you could see his shame for his own answer. For if the Learned Ones could not find it in themselves to trust the man standing before them, why indeed should *anyone*—teacher, rabbi, holy man or mortal—trust *them*?

Eden's master nodded as if he had known as much all along. He quietly replied:

"Then neither will I tell you by what power I do what I do."

And in that moment it seemed to Eden that her master spoke not in anger, but in sadness and regret, that in this matter of belief and authority, trust must take its own time. For only time itself could wear away the hard pit of doubt in these wise men of the temple.

Eden's master joined Judas and Maryam by the stone altar. The two still tugged at the iron chain and collar about the lamb's neck, unable to free the poor creature. But when Eden's master touched the iron band round the tiny lamb's neck, the collar fell away. And he kicked it into the straw.

"I'm free!" cried the littlest lamb as she shook herself, and the other lambs cried back. "I'm free! It's true! I'm free!"

"Yes," Eden told the young lamb. "That much is true. You're free."

Before the companions left the temple precinct, Eden saw the Hollow Man slide out of the shadows. He picked the iron collar off the bed of straw, pondered it for some moments and then looked about the temple compound, searching for another lamb.

I Know Where He Will Be
✳ ✳ ✳

The streets of the city grew quiet, the stalls packed away and their awnings folded. The shop merchants locked their doors and many returned to their homes to prepare for the feast. In the late afternoon the walls were thrown into shadow while a few stragglers scurried along, trying to find shelter before the sun set.

The group passed through the final gate and beyond the city walls.

"Are we going somewhere?" the lamb from the temple altar asked. "Will they feed us? Is this night different from all other nights? Why do we hurry?"

"Perhaps this night is different," Eden told the littlest lamb. "We hurry to get shelter before sunset. But do not fear. Our master has never let us starve, no matter how far we wander."

And when the littlest lamb looked to the donkey, Samson nodded his long gray head. "It is true. We do not go hungry as long as we follow our master's path."

Half a league from the city walls, Judas, the woman named Maryam and the others halted by a cluster of trees in the shoulder of a hill. Eden watched her master speak quietly to his companions. He bid them go no further, but await his return.

Judas drew apart from the others, sitting under heavy

branches. For some moments he muttered to himself, arguing again. Suddenly he rose, hugging his cloak tight about him, his mind made up. Silently he turned from the companions under the trees and headed back to the city walls. Of all the companions only Samson and Eden noticed him go.

Samson looked up from his lambs. "Should we follow him? Do you think he wants company?" the donkey asked.

"He doesn't look lost, but he does look lonely," Eden answered.

"Perhaps he is seeking more lambs to follow us," the littlest lamb suggested.

But Eden shook her head. "Nothing down in the city for you," she told them. "Just empty stone streets and other streets where crowds gather in anger at the world as Romans watch from the walls. If you go back now some soldier will mistake you for the garrison's dinner, and take you away."

The littlest lamb hid behind Samson's legs, abashed. She did not want to be anyone's dinner.

"Don't fret," Samson told her, "nothing will happen to you as long as you do not stray." And Eden thought this the wisest thing she had ever heard the old gray donkey say. Now it was safe enough to leave Samson and his lambs in the stand of trees.

Silently Eden followed Judas down the wooded slope and back to the city.

No one missed them.

The man did not speak but seemed to welcome Eden's company, his loneliness like a heavy cloak. Every few steps he looked down at her as if his final companion might tell him the way. Yet his troubled mind was locked tight against her.

Eden could tell him nothing.

As the late-afternoon shadows crept along the ground before

the city gates they came upon an angry group shouting at the Romans on the parapets above. Eden saw the Hollow Man scuttle from the shelter of the city walls to the safety of the angry rabble. Egging the mob once more, going from one person to another, whispering in their ears or prodding them, urging them, his soft words driving them like animals down the stone streets:

"To the temple!" he hissed. "To the priests! If they don't fear the Romans they should fear you! If they don't fear the Messiah, they shall fear you!"

Judas and Eden fell in among the throngs. At first man and animal were elbowed to the walls. Again someone stepped on Eden's paw and she yelped. But they reached the gates of the temple compound once more. Suddenly Judas veered off, dragging her by the collar. Free of the dangerous crowds he let Eden's collar go, still she hugged his side.

They darted down an empty alley, footsteps echoing off the cobblestones, then turned a sharp corner and halted before the temple compound wall.

No way forward, no way back.

An iron door with an iron grill stood in the stone—a postern door cut into the temple, where those who did not wish to be seen could come and go. Its grill was only wide enough for one face to peer out and one to peer in.

Judas paused. He touched the metal door.

His fingers entwined about the grill and he seemed to hang there for a moment, struggling to breathe.

A few feet away a figure sat cross-legged in the shadows, a beggar. The poor wretch uncovered the rags from his head and stared at Judas by the door. A few coins clinked in his begging bowl.

"You came just in time," the beggar said. He nodded to the high temple wall. "They're waiting. They're expecting you."

Judas stared hard at the creature squatting on the dirty paving stones, then looked away just as suddenly. And Eden knew who spoke from the temple wall. He needed no formal introduction, just as when they had first met on the edge of a cliff in the wilderness. The Hollow Man appeared anytime he wanted, anyplace he wanted. He could be in a thousand places, everywhere and nowhere, and no one could do anything to stop him.

The sound of the crowd rang faintly off the walls. At any moment they might charge around the corner. And suddenly Eden feared the mob would search them out in all their anger, trapping her and Judas in this blind stone alley. The dog could feel the man's troubled mind again, a fierce conflict within: whether to flee this horrible place, flee this creature sitting on the dirty pavement, or—

Seek sanctuary.

Judas knocked on the iron door and the blow echoed faintly into the temple corridor.

A dry voice came from within. "It's open."

Judas pushed the heavy door and its greased hinges made no sound.

The man and the dog stood in a dark stone alcove at whose end stood another gateway whose door was barred like in a prison. Beyond the barred door a single oil lamp burned from a stone niche in a bare chamber, casting more shadow than light. Cloaked priests stood or sat on wooden benches, their faces hidden. Eden couldn't tell how many men, for the shadows beyond the barred gate seemed to hide their number, shifting from one to the next, so that she could not even tell which priest spoke. But she could tell what was true from what was false with each word spoken, as much from Judas as from the men in the bare stone chamber.

"You are from Galilee?" one priest asked.

"Near enough. I have come for the feast," Judas replied. True.

There was a lengthy pause. Then one of the holy men asked: "You follow him?"

"First from the river, almost the beginning." True.

"You witnessed the magic?" another holy man asked.

"I saw what I saw." True.

Then a third priest cleared his throat:

"Will no one among you, will *any of you* who follow him, save him? *Not one?*"

Judas did not answer.

Then another priest with a drier voice:

"Can you not save him from himself?"

Again, Judas did not answer, but shivered inside. True or false?

Could he? Could anyone save their master from himself? He did not know.

"I know where he will be," Judas said at last.

True.

A long silence groped across the dark chamber until it found a resting place.

"That's all we needed," said the dry voice within.

True.

Then after an even longer pause:

"We only wish to save him from himself..."

False.

The empty voices in the stone chamber only wished to save themselves.

There was nothing more to say. Judas retreated out the metal door and Eden heard it shut with a soft metal clang. They stood once more in the blind alley. At their feet lay a small drawstring purse. She sniffed it. Coins.

"Go on," the beggar said. "The ones inside left it for you. Pick it up."

Afraid to touch the ugly purse, Judas took it by the drawstring.

"Bring it here," the poor wretch said. Judas dangled it before the face of the beggar, more than ready to give it to him if only the wretch would reach out and take it. The dirty Hollow Man touched the edges of the purse then drew his fingers away as if unclean.

"No, you found it, you keep it."

Judas hesitated.

"Give it to the others if you want," the beggar man urged. "Your friends need it too."

Judas clutched the body of the purse. *Yes, keep it.*

And the wretch smiled, more satisfied than ever. He presented his begging bowl with a toothless grin. Two stones knocked hollowly in the wooden bowl, a white stone and a black, but neither showed their insides.

"The purse has to be worth more than these," the Hollow Man said with a low chuckle:

"More than my two stones …"

Bread and Wine
✳ ✳ ✳

Judas retreated from the compound walls, down the blind alley, clutching the purse as if it would save him. Out in the street the crowds were still shouting at the temple doors but the man left them to it and Eden followed him toward the city gates.

Once more the two climbed the hill beyond the city walls.

As the dog and the man had not been not missed, only the animals noticed their return. The companions were nowhere to be seen. Samson and the lambs had not moved from the cluster of trees. Quietly, Maryam emerged from the shadows and silently joined them. So only she remained.

"Back so soon?" Samson asked Eden. "What did the man want in the city?"

"He needed to talk to other men," Eden told the donkey. "To trade in words. Some true, some lies."

"Why would he do that?" asked the littlest lamb.

At first, Eden did not know why. But she thought for a moment, of Judas and his cloak of pain.

"To ease his mind," the dog said at last.

"Did it help?" the littlest lamb asked.

Eden only shook her head. "Not that I could see."

The animals fell silent at the sound of approaching footsteps.

A stranger carrying a water jar appeared on the narrow path. The newcomer seemed to know them all, greeting Judas and Maryam with soft words, then pointed up the hill to a cluster of houses. At once everyone began to climb, the animals too, walking up the slope on either side of the rocky path. At length they reached a house. But this was not a dwelling where all could shelter. A flight of stone steps clung to the outer wall. On the landing an open door showed the welcoming light of an upstairs room. Donkeys cannot climb narrow stairs and the lambs were simply too numerous.

But Eden knew how to climb!

The dog bounded behind the Water Jar Man, while Judas and Maryam followed, and the others stayed upon the hillside. Free of the narrow city streets the silly lambs became frisky and boisterous, nosing into the ropes of figs hanging by the house and nibbling at the berries on the bushes against the hillside. Until Samson told them to behave themselves and not to wander off.

Of all the animals only Eden was allowed upstairs that night. Their host put his heavy water jar down and his wife brought a stack of bowls so that all could wash. She even made a nice bed for Eden out of a folded cloak, and set down a dish of water for her to drink. Then silently the Water Jar Wife prepared the feast.

Quietly the others entered as the sun began to set.

When night's shadows darkened the windows the room had filled.

The companions passed around the unleavened bread and poured wine into goblets while Maryam and the Water Jar Wife served. Their master brought a scroll to the table so they might recite, but no one looked at it, as all of them knew the words by heart. Quietly they told the ancient story of bondage to Pharaoh and the flight from Egypt. Yet as they recited the old story of slavery and freedom, they paused in the telling to speak of other matters.

Many things were said that night and many things remembered.

Many things forgotten too, now forever lost.

But most was left unspoken.

Eden had heard the story of hard bondage before, for they told it every year. Dutifully, she tried to listen but gave up, letting the words pass over her head. But as always—when the gift of understanding went away—the smells and scents, the sounds and tastes filled the room.

Stronger now was the food on the table, dates and nuts, chopped apple and honey. She smelled horseradish, an egg with the side of its shell burnt brown, a bit of roasted lamb bone. Before long the Water Jar Wife put a large raw joint in front of her and Eden gave up listening for good.

The ceremony came to an end, the scroll was put away. Maryam and the Water Jar Wife brought to the table the meal of lentils, stewed beef, cheese, olives, and more bread.

Eden stopped working the bone. The table had gone very quiet and her master was speaking, but for some reason his words meant nothing to her. He broke bread once more and offered the pieces to each of his companions. And they took the pieces, the dry scraps of that unleavened bread, as if it meant more to them than any prize, any food, any gift—taking each broken morsel as if it were part of the man himself. And as each companion passed the jagged piece from finger to finger, a few crumbs fell from the table to the floor.

Then Eden watched her master offer his cup from one companion to the next and the wine was passed around once more.

Here again, in their reverence to touch the cup, to drink the wine, their hands trembled and drops spilt as it went from man to man.

What was so special about this bread? Eden wondered. What was so special about this wine? Eden did not know. Still, Eden felt drawn to the fallen crumbs, the drop of wine. She left her bone and went to the spot by her master's chair.

She snuffed the dry crumbs. Just plain bread.

Then the dot of wine. Just wine.

Plain bread. Plain wine. Nothing special. Nothing at all.

Eden felt her master's hand stroke her silken ear. And she loved him back with every fiber of her being and with all her heart. But as the glow filled her, her real age returned like a heavy weight. The moment she loved him back, her magic youth was gone. And suddenly she realized it was him, *her master* who felt old. His burdened mind ran down his arm and into her every string and cord. When his hand finally lifted from her head the connection broke. And her strange wonderful youth returned.

Still one thing bothered Eden, and she thought about it as she worked the bone in her paws, turning it round and round as she gnawed. Not just that her master seemed weary ... but something beyond this upper room. Judas had left the table and gone to the window, staring out into the dark. Eden could feel him gazing down, staring hard toward the city. And she knew his wordless thoughts as though seeing through his eyes.

Watch fires lit the city walls, and in every guardhouse and every keep an oil lamp burned, shining into the night. Upon the bare ground before the gates, people gathered at the end of the feast amongst the hovels of the destitute, those with tents and even those without tents who lived with less than nothing. All the ancient tales had been recited but no one felt their burdens lifted. And now many of the poorest in the city gathered in groups about the gates, crying aloud for one to come to them, to bring them out of bondage as all the tales foretold. Their cries echoed off the city walls and the Roman guards looked down from a great height and with great amusement, for they had beaten this conquered rabble over and over.

Nothing new in any of their pleas.

Except four cups of Passover wine and some stale flat bread in shrunken bellies.

The Roman Governor might sleep tonight, but not his soldiers. Instead the Legionaries would keep a vigil till the dawn broke like a fever, shaking and sweating—and the mob, weary from their struggles, finally crawled into their beds.

Judas gripped the wooden windowsill as if it might steady him. And he muttered, slurring his words together. "Just give us a little time, a little more time—" then tore his eyes from the walls. Judas' mind snapped shut and he let go the wooden sill. When he stopped murmuring he took all his secret thoughts with him and Eden saw no more.

Inside the upper room, Eden's master rose from his seat, and for a moment everyone at the table feared he was going to leave them, walk down the stairs and out to the city walls. Eden saw Maryam's eyes widen in fear, even as the cries down below grew louder, calling for a messiah, a deliverer, anyone to come and save them.

But no one answered the call, not that day.

Eden looked to the spot on the floor where her bone joint waited for her.

But she wasn't hungry anymore.

THE GARDEN
✳ ✳ ✳

Eden followed Judas down the narrow stairs and onto the hillside where Samson and the lambs waited patiently. Nearby the companions talked among themselves. Down from the upper floor, the travelers paused on the rocky slope beside the house of the feast as though unsure where to go. But instead of joining them, Judas sat apart, sitting heavily on a flat boulder beneath a twisted olive tree. He peered ahead, trying to make out the companions' familiar, friendly faces, but the darkness up the hill seemed impenetrable.

Eden tugged the hem of Judas' robe: *C'mon, c'mon, let's go.* But the man seemed too beaten to move.

"No, you go," he told her. "They need you more than me. Go on now."

Reluctantly Eden turned and made her way up the hill leaving Judas by the narrow path. As the darkness closed in around her the last thing she heard was Judas talking to himself, arguing again. The argument was getting worse. But his voice faded, and as she neared the cluster of companions that familiar stealthy padding reached her ears again.

Ah, the fox.

The fox had returned. So he had spoken the truth to them that he would never be far.

Eden

At the doorstep of the house the companions still spoke among themselves, trying to decide where to stay for the night. Samson the donkey looked down his long gray nose at Eden.

"No one can decide where to go," he said. "Some wish to find a safe place on the hillside and others wish to leave the city altogether."

Eden looked suspiciously around. Stay or flee? She didn't know.

"The fox is back."

"Yes, I can smell him."

"Perhaps *he* will find the best place to rest tonight."

"Perhaps," Samson said. "But it won't be with the lambs, they're too noisy. And it won't be with me. Donkeys snore. And a fox won't snuggle up to a dog—you'd only talk all night and then chase him around in circles."

"No," Eden agreed. "In the end I'd only run him down." She put her nose to the ground and snuffed. "And he won't be bothering with the mice either. They have all gone into hiding. No feast for him tonight. He'll go hungry."

"Then why does he follow us?" Samson asked.

"Only he knows," Eden said.

Both the dog and donkey fell silent. Apparently a decision was reached and the companions began to follow their master higher up the slope. Eden and Samson roused the lambs and herded them to follow. Deep in the brush Eden heard the fox pattering along, so he had not given up on them. She almost started to chase him, but that would have meant leaving Samson and the lambs, so she let the fox be.

Suddenly everyone stopped.

They had come to a grove of olive trees, a sheltered garden hidden from the world below. The ground underfoot was soft with moss, the air fragrant, scented with juniper and orange flowers. The squat stone basin of an ancient olive press stood at the edge of the trees. A weary millstone rested in the mill's smooth groove, its stout wooden haft gleamed richly from the grip of nameless hands, olive oil and the turn of countless seasons.

A heavy stillness hung over the garden. The companions rested in the thighs of ancient trunks, the twisted arms of olive branches sheltering their heads. Yet Eden felt no sense of ease. Rather, the dog felt hunted, as if many men were scouring the hills for any sign of their master. Yet none of the others seemed to feel anxious, their eyes heavy with sleep. Only Eden was alert, and this secluded garden no place of rest.

But for the moment no one found them, so the dog watched and waited. Safe for now from the nameless mob, from faceless men in bare chambers, from soldiers combing the rocks and trees. While worse things waited in the dark. And yet Eden felt outcast, an exile, hidden from the troubles down below, guarding those who slept on the last night at the end of the world.

Eden saw her master find a secluded spot away from the others.

He knelt beside an outcrop of rock and began to whisper softly to himself. His murmurs went on and on, rising and falling as though speaking to an unseen listener. And Eden could tell he was pleading with a caretaker she could not see. A great presence who looked down from heaven. Who lived in every olive tree, in every blade of grass. A great seer, the first and last witness, who knew the earth through every creature that crawled or swam or flew, who beheld the world through every living eye and every star in heaven.

He spoke to the Almighty, maker of oceans and mountains, maker of the universe, who saw into the depths of time and the untold future. Eden felt her master's mind begin to break. He balled his hands before his face in prayer. This was *too much* for a single soul to know. Eden could feel his fear, and the demons of fear that preyed on mortal flesh every second of their lives. And her master began to weaken, and to weep, for nothing could stop the night from ending or the sun from coming up.

Of all things he knew, that was the most certain.

Samson joined the dog and then the youngest of the lambs came also, drawn by the sounds of sorrow. They watched their master's whispers escape into thin air, leaving only silence waiting in the shadows of the trees.

Eden became aware of another approaching, their old follower.

The fox padded out of the dark and sat on his haunches by a boulder. He looked from one animal to the next and then back at the man. At first, Eden thought that perhaps the fox was a servant of the Hollow Man, but the fox simply licked his paw and scratched his ear.

"No," he said, reading Eden's mind. "That creature that wears the skin of man does not smell right. I avoid him at all times. And while he has called many of my fellows to his side, none of us go to him. We are creatures of the night, but not of the darkness."

And Eden realized their cautious follower had finally made up his mind, joining them at last. Their master began to whisper again, so faintly only his lips moved. Of all of the creatures, only the fox could hear, for he had the sharpest ears.

"He speaks to the great Beholder," said the fox. "That is why I came, for I know what this means now, whereas before I did not. Perhaps if I stay near, I too will be able to speak to the unseen, and He will listen."

"Who is He?" asked the youngest lamb.

"The same who made us," the wise old donkey told her.

Their master dropped his hands, his face pale as empty parchment. Even in the darkness Eden could see his throat glistened with sweat. A drop rolled down his cheek falling to the ground and left no trace. The air smelled of salt and iron, the scent of life itself.

The air stirred, a fresh breath carrying the scent of jasmine and oranges once more. And the animals felt a presence, not the overpowering Almighty Seer, but of his servant. His messenger, come to earth to do his bidding, emerging from the darkness not as a figure robed in white or some great and powerful voice, but as a calm hand. A hand to strengthen the weak, to banish fear, a hand to lift burdens and let troubles fall away, leaving only strength and mortal will.

All who watched in that green and quiet grove felt it.

First the fox perked his ears, then Eden sniffed the air, then Samson sighed with pleasure and the littlest lamb, last of all, breathed a gentle *bah* ...

The animals shuffled back a step, their own breath and hearts restored.

Their master rose, renewed at last.

He wiped the sweat from his brow, then looked at them, from dog to donkey to lamb, and even out into the darkness where the fox sat near his boulder. Eden's master stood, his weakness gone, standing calmly in the night as if ready for some final task.

And it suddenly occurred to Eden that even though she and Samson and the littlest lamb could not speak human words, they had been blessed by this presence. Surely the others, the travelers who'd been with their master all this time, his companions—surely *they* must feel this too and if they were roused now—*here of all places*—no one would be harmed. The companions would gather about their master and protect him from the world and anyone who sought to do him harm.

Of course, they could. Of course, they would!

She and the donkey, the lambs and even the fox would help. They'd all work together, they'd all protect each other. They'd all protect their master.

But even as she thought this, Eden's blood seemed to pause.

The other animals had suddenly fallen asleep. With nothing to fear there was nothing to keep them awake. Samson nodded his long gray head and snored even though standing up. The youngest lamb, curled on the soft moss, mumbled in her sleep, her little legs twitching in a dream. Even the fox had closed his eyes, breathing heavily in slumber, while sitting. How peculiar. Foxes of all animals would never sleep in the company of others!

What of the companions, certainly none of them would close their eyes?

Eden ran from man to man. One slept heavily in the hollow of a tree trunk, another curled up snoring softly in a bed of grass, and yet another nodded with his head to his knees. *C'mon! Wake up now! Wake up!* She tugged sleeves, the hems of their robes, she nosed one in the face, and snuffed another's ear! But none of them stirred. *C'mon, wake up!*

No use.

Eden ran back to her master and put her head under his hand.

They should have kept awake. They should have stayed with you ...

"In the end, only you kept watch," he told her. "Only you waited through the hour. God's watchful servant. Only you watched with me." He paused, looking at the sleeping forms under the trees. His companions, the travelers, all dead to the world. He looked down at Eden, "Of all of them. Only you. Will anyone remember your name? Anyone but me?"

Eden didn't know. What was in a name, but a sound that you wore like a collar?

Yet when her master spoke the lot of them woke with a start. Suddenly ashamed that they'd fallen asleep, taken a moment's respite and didn't mean at all to leave their master alone. They meant to pray on bended knee just as he did, they meant to …

Eden saw the fox slip away under the brush. His last words almost trailing behind his tail, "Watch out, they're coming! They're almost here!"

Not soon. *Now.*

The sounds of soldiers' feet climbing the hill rose into the grove. The men in armor were searching, the soldiers nearly upon them. They came from below and gathered in a stout knot, blocking any escape. In a moment the peaceful grove was filled with men, spears, swords and shields. They came with torches, and the light shone in every direction. But it was an unhealthy light that made everyone look wan and sick. Eden saw the companions' faces drain of blood, even at night pale fear shone out from every man.

The lambs circled Samson's hooves, awake, confused and bleating, "Who are they? What do they want?" And the littlest lamb, the most fearful of all: "Have they come for me? Are they taking me back to the iron chain?"

The old donkey nuzzled the small creature.

"No, no one comes for us, little one." Samson looked about

at the shivering men who were once their master's most faithful companions, most faithful friends … and then at the stern faces of the soldiers. Eden wondered if the strong donkey was going to turn his hind around and kick. But Samson only shook his long gray head, and muttered, "No good will come of this tonight."

And Eden knew he spoke the truth.

The companion named Judas suddenly reappeared, coming cautiously from behind the squat stone oil press. How long had he been there? How long had he been away? Had he been searching for them all this time? Or had he brought the soldiers from down below? Eden could not tell.

By the light of the soldiers' torches, the spirit of the Hollow Man followed Judas like his own shadow. The troubled companion cautiously crossed the grove, creeping with all the stealth of an animal while the shadow of the Hollow Man twisted this way and that, peering over Judas' shoulder, or leaning away to grope at one companion or the next. The shadow moved of its own accord, a living stain upon the ground. And as Judas moved closer and closer to their master, Eden sensed him struggling to free himself from the dark thing at his feet, struggling and failing and finally giving up.

Now the shadow led him, crossing the grove under the trees. Judas stood before their master, as if to take his hand, to kneel or even kiss his face. Then Judas' dark shadow reached out and even as Eden watched, the dark fingers rose to her master's waist, then to his shoulder. The dark silhouette of a face leaned into his throat like a lover, the shadow leaving a kiss behind, the barest touch on the son of man.

And Judas put his face into his hands, weeping his own tears.

"Oh, still I love thee …" The shadow that pursued him, that clung to him, vanished in an instant. And Judas stood by himself, naked and alone, his soul for all to see. And for a second Eden saw the Hollow Man large as life grinning from the trees. He seemed very pleased with himself, as if this were his finest hour. And as he withdrew into the darkness, only the sickly glow of his smile remained.

Yet another stranger, a servant of the temple, stood in the knot of soldiers.

Then another temple servant joined the first. The servants hesitated as if ashamed, for they had no courage to stand before the torches, but instead cowered beside the armed men, a pair of cowards.

For a moment Eden almost felt sorry for the men …

But before she took another breath, bright metal flashed in the torchlight.

A sword!

The temple servant closest to her cried out and held his head. Shocked, the soldiers brandished their spears. Eden's master looked at the attacker, now kneeling with the sword in his hand, and Eden could see that he was one of their own companions. In an instant the horror of what must happen next flashed through her mind, overwhelming her. For if men spilled blood, certain punishment would follow. Their companion with the sword was a dead man. What other outcome was possible? Knowing his fate, the attacker let the sword loose in his fist and waited for the spears to take his life.

But Eden's master could not let that happen. *No, there would be none of this.* He knelt to the temple servant clutching his head, making sure the wounded man would live.

"Put up your sword," he whispered to his foolish friend.

No, neither man would not die this day. Neither companion nor temple servant.

Instead, their master offered himself to the soldiers of his own free will.

He opened his palms accepting his fate.

Without warning the soldiers moved as one thrall. The men whipped the donkey and Samson brayed. Eden leapt away to avoid the booted feet, and the lambs scattered in every direction. The last thing Eden saw: her master stumbling down the hill between soldiers with spears and shields, and many rough hands upon him.

They knew the man they dragged down the hill.

Everyone knew.

No need to look further tonight.

At last they had found him.

Denial
✳ ✳ ✳

At this hour and in the midst of the darkness Eden sat quietly beside a black stone. The soldiers' commotion faded down the hill. The stealthy fox twitched his whiskers as he sat nearby, but Eden made no effort to chase him. He looked at her then shook his head sadly. "I thought that after drawing this close, I could learn to speak his name. But nothing has changed in me and still I cannot. I am just a fox with a fox's tongue."

Samson clopped about in the dark among the stones, searching out one lamb and then another and then another. He used his long gray nose to nestle them close. In a few moments they had gathered back to him under the branches of the olive trees.

"What do we do now?" cried the littlest lamb.

"Yes, what do we do now? What now?" the other lambs cried.

But for once Samson had no answer.

The donkey looked to Eden as if the dog could tell him.

"Wait here," she told Samson and his lambs.

"I shall follow the men, for I must know where they go."

Eden had no trouble tracking the soldiers, for a rank odor from their smoky torches hung in the air marking a trail down the hillside. In the wide courtyard of a grand house a fire burned in a fire pit, lighting the compound walls. The soldiers guarded the main doors of the house, while servants and travelers gathered around the fire pit seeking warmth and shelter.

The soldiers had brought her master into the large house of the chief priest himself. Eden heard the voices of other men rising and falling faintly within. The men of the temple were putting questions to her master as once they had before, but this time the voices were harsher than the Learned Ones in the temple who wished only understanding and wisdom. These were more challenges, not reverential, nor with any hint of a desire for knowledge or a need to know. And it seemed to Eden the harsh voices didn't really want replies from her master—only to put angry questions riddled with fear.

Eden's sharp ears heard other voices too, scratchy little voices. A pack of rats crouched in the dark of the house wall. They had watched her master go inside the house and laughed at his silence as the endless questions rained down.

"Oh, they've got him, all right," the Chief Rat said.

"Yes, with testimony," another chattered. "That he would tear down the temple with his bare hands!"

"No, no!" squealed another rat, "Now another witness has a different story. This one says that he would build it again, but not with his hands."

The rats were confused for no one could agree what was said, or who said it or what was truly meant by it all, and for several moments they scurried about in the shadow of the house walls, lashing each other with their tails in frustration.

At last the Chief Rat said, "Now they are demanding to know whose son he really is." The Chief Rat took a big breath, smiling behind his teeth. "He won't even say that," the Chief

Rat gloated. "No, he won't say it. But they say *they heard* him say it. Oh, they've got him good now."

"Yes," the others cried in their scratchy voices, "they've got him good." And the pack of rats all rubbed their little claws together in delight. In that moment of triumph and jubilation the Chief Rat's beady eyes latched on to Eden. And the pack held their breath, wondering whether to stand or flee. The Chief Rat scuttled along the wall, his red beady eyes challenging her, and others followed. Safety in numbers.

"Did you not know him?" the Chief Rat demanded. "Was he not your master from birth? Did you not know him better than anyone here?"

At first Eden did not know what to say. Was this low creature worth answering?

But dogs cannot lie. And even rats deserve an answer.

Of course, Eden knew him. Everyone knew her master.

Too bad this ugly rat didn't know him—it might have done him good.

She stared grimly at the Chief Rat, her lip raised, wondering whether it would be better just to grab him by the neck and shake him to death.

But then the strangest thing happened. A familiar smell touched Eden's nose, a scent from within this courtyard.... *Ahhh*, one of their master's companions huddled by the fire. One of the first gathered back by the banks of the river. The fisherman who cast nets upon the sea, the one named Peter. Long had he followed her master's footsteps from village to field, and slept beside the lambs in every orchard. This companion was always kind to her, but Peter talked more to men than he ever did to animals. Now sitting before the fire pit in the courtyard of this grand house he hugged his knees to his chest, staring hard into the flames. Every so often he looked nervously about as if listening for some signal. The dog could tell he strained his ears to the thick walls, laboring to hear everything that was going on beyond the bolted doors.

But even as the voices died within, one voice from the fire pit demanded:

"Did you not know him? Were you not his friend?"

Everyone staring into the fire went silent, waiting for an answer. And Eden realized that Peter's mind *was not* troubled like either Judas or Maryam, but frozen from within, *petrified* like the salt statues by the great dead water. Now he cowered under the shadow of the Hollow Man—making his denial all the more shameful.

This companion's voice so soft Eden could barely hear it:

Not I, he swore, *not I.*

But what the dog saw on his face was worse.

The one named Peter shrank inside himself.

Wishing only to disappear.

To be gone and never have been born.

A cock on a rooftop crowed—the first herald of sunrise—for somewhere over the horizon the bird could feel the dawning of a black day.

At that very moment, the doors of the great house opened and the soldiers prepared to bring Eden's master forth, and the travelers and those who sought shelter rose and fled the fire's light. All those who waited scuttled into the shadow of the walls. The rats screamed as they were stepped on. The Chief Rat ran into the first crack in the wall he could find, tail wriggling in fear as it disappeared into the stone.

But Eden caught him by the tail, and dragged him from the wall. She shook him, his shrill squeals echoing in the courtyard.

And when the Chief Rat went limp in her teeth, Eden spat his body out.

Let the Romans Decide
✳ ✳ ✳

Dawn broke against the high walls of the city, an overcast, ugly day. Damp clouds blew across the rooftops, smelling of rust and ash. The sun slid into the gray metal sky and Eden felt a great weight overhead, gazing down with hooded eyes. After the cock crowed in the courtyard of the grand house no birds chimed in, no starlings chirruped, no doves cooed in the corners of the houses.

Eden noticed a scrawny cat slinking along an open drain at the side of the road.

The cat halted to wipe her face with her paws.

"Where are the mice?" the cat asked of no one.

Looking about again she shook her head. "No mice. All hiding, all gone."

A kind of horrible quiet descended on the world, a dawn like no other the dog had ever seen. The silence broken only by the muffled stamp of the soldier's feet as they marched Eden's master toward the city.

At the base of the hill she was surprised to find Samson waiting with the littlest of the lambs by a deserted crossroads. *Why did you leave the safety of the garden?* she almost growled.

But the growl died on her tongue as she saw what the two animals were looking at. A withered, wretched tree with a man hanging by his neck, a common enough sight this close to the city walls, and the soldiers marched their master past without a second glance.

But Eden knew whose legs dangled dead off the ground. She knew that sandal, fallen from his foot. How could she not have known Judas was dead? She should have missed his living mind. She should have known if only because she knew the man.

A long thread of sweat had rolled down his leg and clung to his bare heel.

"We found him this morning," Samson told her. "The littlest one told me there was a lost lamb down below, and we came in search of it. Not a lamb, *a man*. We would have brought Judas back with us to the garden. We might have helped him. But we came too late. Too late."

Eden didn't know what to say. She never thought the one named Judas a bad man, but the troubles of his mind devoured him and now this was all that remained. Perhaps the littlest lamb and the donkey were right; perhaps Judas was like a lost lamb. In the gray light of morning his body did not cast even a shadow. She sniffed the sandal on the ground, but all she smelled on it was grit and dust and sorrow. Eden noticed a threadbare pouch lying at the base of the tree. A few silver coins spilled from the purse's mouth and beside the coins two pebbles, a black pebble and a white one, lying on the ground. The Hollow Man had done his work well, taking the human being, the earthly Judas, and leaving only the purse behind.

But even as Eden stared at the abandoned purse a beggar pushed Eden aside, stooped to the ground and snatched the coins. The wretched creature clutched the purse to his chest, and hurried after the Romans approaching the city. He threw a grin over his shoulder as he ran toward the city walls. And Eden recognized him again. Who else? The Hollow Man.

The soldiers were crossing the threshold of the city now, marching under the gate.

"Samson!" Eden cried. "We're too late for this poor man, we can do nothing here. But there goes our master. We can't let him get away."

"I'm afraid," said the littlest lamb. But both her guardians herded her close.

"You're with us," Eden said.

"And even though this is no day to travel alone," Samson told her, "no harm will come to you."

"Come, little one," Eden told the littlest lamb, "our day is not done. If there is someone to be saved, we must see to it." Suddenly they realized the soldiers had disappeared into the city. Samson hesitated, for he could not see very far ahead.

"Follow me," Eden told the other two. "I'll know where he goes. I'll know our master's scent even if he's on the other side of the world."

The three animals followed the soldiers' footsteps over the hard paving stones. The streets ran off in every direction, bewildering the eye, but Eden kept them true.

There seemed to be no end of the poor and wretched in this city. They gathered in every alley, in every street. No end to beggars, to thieves, to all the angry unfortunates gathered in one cramped place. Some reached out to grab the animals, the littlest lamb especially, but Samson's great girth shoved the hungry ones off and Eden only had to raise her lip to keep the famished and the truly desperate away.

At a cross street the unruly crowd had pinned a woman

against a wall, and she struggled to keep from being crushed, crying, "Stop! Stop please, stop!"

Maryam!

The woman who once spoke to flies recognized her animal friends at once, desperately reaching out before being shoved against the wall again. But the three creatures wouldn't stand for this any longer. Samson planted himself against the mob while Eden stood underneath him, raising her lip again and again, keeping the worst ones away. The littlest lamb pressed herself to Maryam's side, nuzzling the woman with her soft muzzle.

After a few moments the crowd backed off. And the people muttered among themselves to see such a strange thing, dumb beasts protecting this lost soul huddled in the street. Maryam petted the littlest lamb, stroked Eden's strong neck and patted Samson's wide flank.

"Oh it's so good to see you all! Eden, I was afraid I'd never see you again. Oh Samson, how strong you are! And little lamb, never leave my side and I'll never leave yours."

The animals nestled close to Maryam, protecting her. And the woman took Eden's face in her hands. "Do you know where they took him? Can you lead us there?"

As Samson couldn't speak to people, he just nodded his big gray head. *Eden knows, she knows.* And Maryam understood. Looking fearfully over the donkey's back she saw the crowd had calmed at the sight of the animals' strange behavior, at this strange sight of a dog, a donkey, a woman and a lamb huddled as one.

At last they moved—dog, donkey, woman and lamb cautiously leaving the safety of the wall. People gaped at this strange procession. Word of them rippled ahead on a thousand whispers and people backed away, the crowd parting as Eden's nose led them on.

The soldiers had brought their master round a corner, down a back alley and to the rear of the garrison. Eden seemed to know this place, like an old memory hiding in her bones. The garrison had a familiar smell, though she had never been here before. Yet somehow she knew it as a place where dogs guarded the men who guarded other men. Not a good place, but a place where many came to die.

Suddenly Samson shivered down to his hooves. "Oh, let us get away from here," he said. "Let us get away. This is where my *own master* died. This is where they brought the River Man before the end."

But Eden couldn't leave. Not yet. And Maryam, unafraid, knelt against the prison wall, placing her hands upon the stone, her face against the mortar. The great stones of the garrison were black. Smudged from endless traffic, from smoky oil lamps, rubbed dark by desperate prayers, countless vigils and blackened from within by a thousand years of cruelty harder than the hardest heart.

Maryam shifted her hands to a cleaner spot, a paler stone, bleached white from the sun, and pressed the stone with all her might. Then lovingly stroked the block, making it speak to her. Cocking her head, she listened.

"I can hear inside," she told the animals. "They have him there. Shall I tell you what they say?" She listened to the great blocks of stone in the wall. Her lips moved, and she spoke, telling all of what she heard:

"These men do not care whether he lives or dies. They have brought him for questions because the priests are afraid of the people they serve. But the priests in the temple mistake fear of their people as fear of God." She took a deep breath and pressed her hands to the stone. "Now they put the question. *Is he the son of man or the son of God—or both?*"

She held her breath, listening to the stone.

"Well, what does he say?" asked the littlest lamb.

For some time Maryam said nothing.

Then quietly:

"I can barely hear ..." Her hands rubbed and rubbed the pale stone. "Wait!" She strained to hear. "He answers. *You say I am. You say it.*"

"The Governor of this garrison is sitting in judgment. I can feel the Roman thinking ... *this man is the son of no one. If he were my son, I'd have taken him from his mother and sent him into the Legions long ago. He's as harmless as a fly. And these priests are old women, afraid of their own shadows.*

"Ah ... the Governor is speaking now. Someone else is to

decide." Maryam took her face from the wall and looked at the animals. "They're taking him to Herod."

"Who's Herod?" asked the littlest of the lambs.

"One of the men who rules this terrible land," the woman answered.

"Did he put me on the chain?" asked the littlest lamb.

"No," Maryam told her. "But he wouldn't have cared if you died there."

She sagged from the stone, exhausted.

The pale stone she had been rubbing with her hands had shown its insides. The white dust rubbed away now showed its beneath, and its beneath was black. Maryam touched her face to brush away sweat. The black from the stone smudged her forehead, the black from the stone blackening her hands.

"Stand back," she told the animals. "Don't let them notice us. They're coming."

Maryam and the animals followed the Roman soldiers at a safe distance. The Legionaries didn't seem to care about them, just the man in their midst as he stumbled along. He tripped once, making his guards bump into him, and one of them struck out with the flat of his sword to get him moving again.

Eden and Samson and the littlest lamb felt the clouds overhead frowning in anger, as though kneaded by great hands, torn and knotted together again. Maryam glanced fearfully up at the sky, but it glowered down and she shielded her head with her scarf.

After a few turns and down an empty street they reached a palace not far from the garrison. They could tell it was a palace because of the brightly tiled walls and the lush, green plants hanging from every terrace. The walls glistened where servants had overwatered the flowers and vines in streams running down the bright tiles, as if the palace wept.

Even at this morning hour sounds of music and carousing reached the animals' ears, the continuation of a great party that had been going on all night. Thus now at dawn, the water streaks on the palace walls looked like tears of laughter. As the soldiers entered the hanging gardens, the music faltered and died. Suddenly servants thrust open the palace doors.

Maryam became quietly afraid. She crouched by the outer wall and peered into the courtyard, the animals crowded beside her. Samson guarded her back, the littlest lamb at her feet, and Eden planted herself at the woman's side so no one might approach her.

The revelers emerged from the inner rooms. A gaggle of palace courtiers lurched drunkenly through the doors followed by musicians carrying their drums and flutes, women clutching any man they could find. The nobles and retainers stood about, amused, expectant. The elders of the temple had also joined everyone that morning and stood in a line like crows on a wall, dourly looking on, sour and sober. No, none of them had been drinking all night. The Romans in their red cloaks pushed the man out from among them and he stood in the cold light of dawn, silent and alone.

Finally the Prince of the palace emerged from the inner doors. His wine-soaked eyes looked from face to face innocently, pretending he did not know whom the soldiers brought before him.

At the palace wall, Maryam knelt and clutched Eden to her breast. The dog could feel the woman's heart pounding and the woman's terrible fear, even her thoughts. *If the priests in their grand house could not decide what to do, how could this king with his sodden courtiers and tipsy ladies know?*

"Why does that prince want to talk to our master?" asked the littlest lamb.

Eden could smell the perfumed drunkard from the shadow of the courtyard wall. And just as with Maryam, the dog felt the drunkard's mind consumed with a fire of questions. The Prince was a trivial man, cowering inside his kingly robes, afraid like everyone else. Yet Eden saw deeper. His greedy, purple-stained lips hungered for legitimacy.

Virtue.

And this besotted Prince in his kingly robes had none.

Yet here was some obscure fellow the mob called a king, a lowly man who stood before a true prince in that noble's own palace garden.

Had this preaching fool no palace to call his own?

"Who is the King they bring to me?" the wine-faced Prince asked. "Is this the King foretold?" The bejeweled Prince peered at the man standing before them, then stared conspicuously about the palace garden as if to find another king in their midst. He smiled knowingly at the elders of the temple, daring them to speak.

The Prince's eyes gravely returned to the man at hand.

Mocking:

"*This man? This is the one* my father feared?"

The elders of the temple all began to talk at once, angry voices accusing the man of every vice, every sin, every crime— but the Prince held up a hand for silence. He approached cautiously and touched the frayed sleeve of the man's ragged shirt, then quietly asked, "Did you know my father?"

He waited for an answer but when none came, the Prince spoke again:

"They say you were born in Bethlehem. My father knew the children of Bethlehem. In my father's day some old wanderers called it the Town of the Star for a child they sought. A Usurper. So my father cleansed the town of all like you. Today the children of Bethlehem may be older or younger, but none of your age. Are you this Usurper? If you survived the Cleansing of Bethlehem, then *truly a miracle* you stand here today."

Maryam clutched Eden's neck, and the dog could feel the woman: *Just speak, say something, do anything. Show them. They'll bow down now. If you just show them the slightest sign. Please. Now. Do it now.*

Nothing happened. Their master stood silently in the tiled courtyard surrounded by the leering courtiers, the loose women and the dour priests ruffling their robes like a row of fussy crows. Then the Prince searched the elegant sash about his waist and drew from the folds a threadbare purse. He showed the purse to the crowd gathered in the garden. The coins inside clinked faintly.

"Silver," the Prince chuckled. "One of my retainers found this purse not far from the city walls. Silver coins at the feet of a dead man hanging in a tree."

No one spoke. The silence pressed down on the courtyard. Eden saw a familiar face again, standing among the others. No longer a beggar, the Hollow Man wore the embroidered cloak of a courtier.

At last the Prince addressed their master:

"Your young friend took the silver in exchange for you. Then took his life. He even tried to return this silver, but no one seems to want it back."

Eden

The ragged man made no reply.

"Let the Priests decide what to do with their silver." The Prince tossed the purse towards the line of dour men. The dark birds ruffled their feathers and let it fall. The purse spilt coins, the line of men trembled at the sight of the silver—but no one stooped to pick it up. Better to wait when no one would see.

But the young Prince of this palace garden was not yet through.

He needed to know more.

"But what of the other tales we've heard?" he asked. "Surely you can show us something."

Again their master spoke no word.

For a moment Eden feared the wine-soaked Prince would anger, but he only scoffed. Just as with the purse, the Prince showed his guests what he held in the palm of his hand. The Prince gazed wistfully at the ragged man standing in the courtyard, then offered him the two stones:

"They say you carried these two stones, and that by holding these two stones a man can know every human heart. Is that true?"

Eden felt Maryam grip tightly around her neck, *say something, anything.*

"It shouldn't be too hard to tell what's in my heart," the Prince said softly.

"Can you tell?" he asked.

But when their master remained silent the Prince sighed and shook his head. The line of temple elders scowled and began to caw. The Prince glared them to silence and snorted in contempt:

"You're afraid of *him*?"

The dour line of black-robed men drew their cloaks about them and fell to whispers.

Finally there was nothing more to say, nothing more to do. The worldly Prince had come with questions and none were answered. Now he tired of the game. He shrugged.

"So be it."

The Prince let the two stones drop from his hand. From their place at the gate neither the animals nor the woman could tell whether the insides were white or black. For when they fell, the two stones broke to pieces, no black, no white, nothing but fragments on the courtyard tiles.

"At least do not depart my house the beggar you appeared," the Prince told Eden's master. "We can find you a robe, I imagine." He took a worn robe from one of his guards and draped it about the man's shoulders.

"Perhaps someone else will find you a crown."

To the temple elders he said:

"Behold, your King."

And then to the gathered company:

"Pilate is in charge of the prison. Let the Romans decide."

Again, the animals and Maryam followed at a distance. With each step onlookers seemed to spring from the very street, until a mob crowded the pavement stones. Maryam and Samson were elbowed aside, while underfoot Eden and the littlest lamb were stepped on. Eden kept seeing the Hollow Man slipping in and out of the crowd. For a moment beside a beggar, then beside a merchant, then hiding behind the skirts of a housemaid, never in one place for long, but traveling along with everyone like the shadows on their feet.

Eden nudged Maryam to warn her of the dark man's

presence, but the woman didn't need to be told. "I see him," she said.

"I see him too," said Samson.

"And me as well," said the littlest lamb. "Don't lose me."

The Roman soldiers marched their prisoner back toward the Governor's court of law, not inside the garrison but to a narrow paved plaza under high stone walls. The mob gathered at an iron gate and shouted over each other's heads. A sea of angry faces: angry at the Romans, angry at the leaden sky, angry at each other. Scattered drops of rain fell.

A few cool drops, but not enough to calm fevered heads.

And this angered them even more.

The three animals and the woman shrank into a corner—they could see and hear but get no closer than the rabble. As before, Samson the donkey shielded Maryam and the smaller ones from heedless feet with his broad flanks. The woman clutched the old donkey's neck as angry men approached with ropes to drag him off, but Samson brayed and Eden bared her teeth and the men dared come no closer.

"Why are they here? What are they doing?" bleated the littlest lamb.

"Why are these people so angry?" she asked.

"What has our master done to make them so?"

But neither Eden nor Samson knew the answer.

Since dawn they had been caught up in the angry crowd, taken from the garrison to the palace and now back to this stone plaza. At each place pushed and shoved and even clawed at, all because they dared follow a man they knew. Trapped as they were they could move no farther. Maryam's face pressed against the nearest wall, streaked with dirt. She pressed her hands against it also, as though to will her body through the stone, but to no avail.

These blocks would not let her see through them.

And Eden saw her sag in defeat.

Suddenly a chorus of voices cried, "He's here! He's here!"

Faces swarmed the iron gate.

Their master had entered the enclosure.

Now the mad rabble clutched one another, some in fear, but many more in eagerness, loving the spectacle of this ragged man standing on the well-laid stones before the seat of power.

Sentries guarded every corner, and others had arrived to witness judgment. The Prince of the hanging garden waited under an awning along with the elders of the temple. The head Roman came out through an open door. He paused for a moment to speak with the Prince of the palace. The Prince wore bright new robes, but dark circles ringed his eyes and he seemed a little shaky. The two nobles nearly touched heads, as a few words passed between them. The Prince fawned, grateful for the slightest nod from the Roman Governor. And the Governor shrugged in return, satisfied the Prince knew his place.

The head Roman took a seat before the prisoner and glanced disparagingly at the bearded elders of the temple. They stood a few paces away and he wanted them no closer.

Servants brought out a low footstool and placed it at the Roman's feet. Rich, embroidered and bejeweled clothes were laid upon the stool; and Eden could see the temple elders touch each other's hands in fear, in anticipation ... and something else. Lust. The elders clucked their tongues, one or two reaching out in anguish for the vestments on the footstool. If only they could touch them, if only they could wear them, if only—

The Roman Lord barely gave the holy men another glance,

and casually signaled the servants to approach. He offered his booted feet to his slaves, and the servants dutifully unlaced his soldier's boot, rimed with city dirt. The Roman Lord sighed as the boot came away and he rested his naked foot upon the footstool, upon the fair, embroidered robes. The temple elders gasped as one, too afraid to move.

Then he offered his other soldier's boot to be removed.

And dutifully the servants kneeled, and tugged the laces.

This then, is how it was to be, Eden realized.

This then, was the master of the world, showing he could do what he wanted, to whomever he wanted—whether it be prince, priest, or ragged man who stood before him, waiting for his will.

All lay beneath his feet.

Eden heard the Roman Lord's voice as it escaped through the barred gate:

"Behold a man." He paused and looked at the elders of the temple. *"This one?"*

They assented, one head bobbing after the next.

The Roman Lord grunted. "I find no fault in him."

The elders let up a protest, the squawk of birds.

The Roman Lord raised his hand for silence and then addressed their master:

"We meet again."

Eden wished her master to reply, even just to say, hello. But he made no sound, and the Roman Lord grew stern.

"So I ask once more … where art thou from?"

But their master held his tongue. No answer for the seat of judgment.

The Roman Lord shifted his feet upon the temple vestments.

"I have the power to hurt thee. I have the power to crucify thee. But I also have the power to release thee."

Eden watched the Roman Lord look to the temple elders, then to the Prince standing in the shadow of the awning. The people watching under the high stone walls seemed to shudder within themselves and pressed their bodies to the iron gates. Eden could see the Hollow Man again. As in the garden he went amongst the people as a shadow. But even in the guise of a formless stain, he was doing what he always did, floating from person to person, slouching through the crowd, slipping past this one, sidling up to another, and in each ear his shadow paused to whisper. Whispering just a single word … and Eden strained to hear this special word.

Then it came to her, floating on dark lips. *Punish.*

The shadow was urging every ear to punish the man. Whispering, *punish, punish* … Punish him.

But the shadow of the man did not touch every ear, for it was important to sow discord. Many in the crowd sought mercy while others sought a reckoning. The crowd fought against itself. This was important too, that some might cry for mercy and not be heeded. That mercy should be offered, but then *denied.*

How Eden could know all this she did not understand, but these complicated human thoughts flowed into her head unbidden. She saw the soldiers and the Roman Lord in the stone plaza, stern and unforgiving. She saw the temple elders, lined up like the poor caged birds that once filled the temple enclosure. She even saw the bejeweled palace Prince whose father had once murdered infants, all except her master. The Prince gazed dimly from under the awning aware of this miracle, at this grown man, now standing before them.

All this she saw.

Samson standing stoically, Maryam frozen in fear and clutching the littlest lamb, and even this tiny creature not daring to move lest some evil member of the crowd notice how pretty she was and take her for her fleece.

Suddenly, Eden saw the shadow cross the pavement. Now it wrapped itself around the littlest lamb and Eden heard it whisper into the lamb's soft ear:

The more things get complicated, the less reliable they are. A lamb rules nothing. Not even other lambs.

At this the littlest lamb shook her head and Maryam frantically brushed away the shadow that lay across her fleece to rid them of this awful presence. And Eden leapt into the space with the stain upon the pavement, but there was nothing there. The shadow had moved on, pouring poison into one ear and then the next. And into each ear it touched, the shadow spoke a single word. The word was "crucify." Crucify. *Crucify.*

For a moment the crowd paused, ignoring the shadow in their midst. For their rulers were offering them a role in these proceedings, a chance to decide the fate of one wretch over another. At this very moment, the choosing made a difference. The Roman Lord was asking a question of everyone within the sound of his voice. "This man or *this one*?" he demanded, peering across the plaza.

The soldiers had brought out yet another prisoner, this one beaten to his knees.

"Your King, the anointed one? Or this zealot, this rebel who plots rebellion in every cellar and sewer ... Barabbas? You choose. Their fate is up to you."

Hair hung before the prisoner's downcast eyes, a bandit without a future, a murderer without hope. If he had even heard the Roman Lord speak, he made no sign. The raised hand of justice bid the people choose between the men. The rebel or the king?

The crowd muttered in answer, a confused mix of voices. Some thought the king should be spared, others the rebel, and the sound rose to a crescendo of noise. The low crowd settled on one and not the other. Wishing the notorious rebel spared, chanting his name over and over:

"Bah-Rah-Bas—! Bah-Rah-Bas—!"

Was there ever any doubt? The shadow had done its work too well.

Their master would go to his last place on earth. The bandit Barabbas would go free.

The Roman Lord dipped his hands into a bowl held by a servant, and water ran down his fingers onto the pavement. Eden watched her master. His cracked lips begged with thirst, but there was no water for him. Instead, the Roman soldiers led the wretched man out the iron gate and up the street.

The one called Barabbas scurried from the stone plaza almost on their heels. A look of terror in his eyes, terror that he no longer had to face that word the crowd chanted over and over—crucify. *Crucify.* His eyes streamed with tears of joy that he was free, and tears of panic that somehow they would snatch his freedom from him. *Freedom. Freedom.* He'd been condemned along with that crazy one standing before the Roman Lord—but now he was *free*. And the crowd chanted, "Go now! Go! You're free! You're free!"

The freed prisoner paused for a moment as some from the crowd touched his rags. Then for another moment he paused before the animals, paused and knelt to Eden, reaching out his hands to her. And for once, Eden did not want to raise her lip.

"The Roman Lord didn't want me," he said to the dog.

"Instead they brought the water bowl," the man cried. "He washed his hands," he gasped. "I'm free!"

"Like me," the littlest lamb said. But the crowd surrounded the prisoner and swept him down the street with cheers of acclaim and adulation, following the Romans as they marched their master out of sight. And when Eden looked back into the stone plaza the Roman Lord's clay bowl had been dropped, broken on the pavement, and the puddle of water ran into the cracks.

INRI

✸ ✸ ✸

The narrow streets were crowded and smelled of dung. Eden caught the scent she knew so well and never lost it—*her master up ahead*. The donkey followed, the tiny lamb trotting next and the woman last, hurrying to catch him once more. The pursuers hugged the walls and doorways so as not to be drawn back into the crowd.

After a few turns they saw their master struggling on. The man moved slowly, step by step, for he was burdened and the crowd taunted him. His cloak askew, his shirt in tatters, and blood seemed to be leaking from every tear in the cloth. He dragged the great beam of wood they used to kill men and he shuddered every time one of the Romans touched him with the switch.

Eden watched him step after step, holding back along the walls so as not to overtake him. Along the way the soldiers had made a crown for him of twisted briers. They placed the thorns upon his head.

A real king now.

His naked feet stepped in drops of his own blood fallen from his brow. Eden could smell the whiff of iron every time a drop struck the paving stones. Spilled blood always had the tang of iron in it. But as the rabble hovered beside him, foot after foot smudged the stain into the pavement and the metallic whiff disappeared so there was no telling blood from dirt.

And something new touched Eden.

She felt her master's body, every joint and every sinew. The strength of her limbs faded and weakness enveloped her like that tattered cloak clinging to her master's shoulders. Her head grew faint, her legs feeble. Her paws ached with every step. She looked fearfully at Samson to see if he felt the weakness too, and then to the littlest lamb and Maryam, but they showed nothing except the need to follow in his steps.

Eden watched her master stumble, the large wooden beam pressed him down to the ground, and the donkey trotted forward as if to help. Yes, Samson wanted to help, the large wooden beam wouldn't be hard for him to carry, if someone would but strap it to his back. This was what Samson was made for, to carry other's burdens. And even the littlest lamb trotted closer too, crying, "I can help. Let me help!"

But in that moment, many hands reached out for the gray old donkey and the pretty lamb, hands that sought to throw a rope about Samson's neck, hands that sought to snatch the littlest lamb away. Eden was torn—follow their master as he stumbled forward or rush to Samson and the lamb?—*what to do, what to do?*

A Roman boot kicked her and she yelped, then was thrown against the woman. Maryam clutched Eden's head to her breast. And the dog watched helplessly as the crowd tried to catch the donkey, the littlest lamb hiding under his strong belly. Samson kicked and two men went down, he kicked again and three men went down. With the last kick he bolted away, and the littlest lamb scampered after him leaving five men groaning in the street. No one else chose to follow. There was a better show only a few paces away.

Maryam clutched Eden's sagging neck.

"Come," she whispered hoarsely, "we can't give up now."

Above them the clouds loomed from horizon to horizon, an angry leaden sky. A few drops of rain pattered down, changing nothing.

Everyone knew where they were going.

Everyone knew the name of this hill.

The Skull. For the place stood out like the crown of a bald head. Panting as they climbed, Maryam fell to her knees, scraping the dirt. She rose up with an old white shard of pottery in her fingers. No, not whitened clay ... *bleached bone in her hand.* But bone of what creature, animal or man? She shuddered and dropped it in disgust.

"King David, King of the Jews!" Maryam swore. She paused to catch her breath, explaining to Eden, "They say King David buried Goliath's head in this hill." The woman began to climb once more. "Goliath forever staring out of this ground."

But Eden needed no name, no story.

The ground itself spoke to her. Bones of the dead poked from the earth, and along the climb the shreds of men hung from trees. Just as Eden had seen on every road she traveled, nameless, forgotten men unworthy of their own wooden beam. For not every criminal or common man merited a cross. Here on this Hill of the Skull, countless white shards hastily buried emerged from the dirt, but no bones that Eden cared to touch.

Their master dragged his wooden beam over the final ruts to the crest.

The crowd had thinned. The cripples and beggars and pickpockets had no heart to climb from the dell before the city gates, but Eden and Maryam struggled on in the soldiers' steps.

What of Samson and the littlest lamb? Eden suddenly wondered. The two had run off, chased by men. Had they outrun them? Would they ever meet again? The question sat in Eden's mind but shrank each step she climbed. And at last her master and the soldiers cleared the crest and the great wooden beam reached the flat summit.

Others had preceded them, two other prisoners with wooden beams.

And more soldiers with picks and shovels.

The grunts of the Legionaries filled the air as they cleaned out old post holes with their sharp spades. Her master lay on his narrow rail, arms outspread, too beaten from his stumbling path through the city to make a sound, too weary from his climb to struggle. As Eden and the woman watched they heard the clink of hammer and nail. But not through flesh. A Roman soldier, wearing no armor but his carpenter's apron, hammered a wooden panel over their master's head. A written word was scrawled on the plank:

INRI.

Eden couldn't read. Nor could she understand the minds of others in this place of death, or even know what her master was thinking. There was no thinking, there was only pain and defeat. Maryam clutched Eden by the neck afraid to let go, and the dog felt the anguish pulsing from the woman with each pound to the spike.

At last the soldier carpenter put down the hammer.

"There," he proclaimed. "Yashua, that's your name, isn't it? That's what people call you, isn't it? *Joshua?*" But the man did not reply. The Roman looked to the onlookers gathered on the hill's crest, "He's from Nazareth, no? Is no one here from Nazareth?" Again none of the onlookers answered.

"Well, our Lord Pilate says he was of Nazareth. I think it reads better in Latin, a civilized language. IESVS NAZARENVS REX IVDÆORVM," he said boldly. "Iesus, Nazarenus … Rex Iudaeorum.… But we can write it in Hebrew if you like. Even Greek." The Roman soldier threw a scornful glance down at the broken man. "But just so all here can understand—Jesus of Nazareth, King of the Jews. So says Lord Pilate."

As if in answer, the groans of two others perched on their wooden crossbeams filled the air, but no one paid attention. All manner of sounds lived on this hill of the skull. The clink of shield and spear, the grunts of rough men settling in for a long wait, the creak of ropes, even the slosh of water from water jars brought for everyone but the condemned.

And there was one last crossbeam to set upright.

With stout rope, thoroughness and care the soldiers tied their master's arms from shoulder to elbow to the wood; no man was allowed to peel off the cross before his time. The rope would let him hang.

Then came the iron spikes. Two sharp cries as each spike nailed the wrists. It took many hands to lift the man, to plant the base of his rail into the waiting hole. And he cried out a third time as the base of the beam struck bottom. Mallets drove wedges into the ground and packed the dirt tight. The beam stood firm.

The Roman soldier who had hammered the sign took off his carpenter's apron, folded his hammer and nails into the leather and tied the thongs. He glanced up at the last prisoner, the man from Nazareth mounted on his beam:

"This be a king? A king to all men?" the Roman carpenter scoffed. He wagged his head in scorn. "Bow to a king like him, then Rome shall rule eternal."

His fellow soldiers grunted in agreement.

"If he's all things to all men, then he's really nothing to no one."

And the others laughed.

Eden looked about for the Hollow Man; for this was the kind of thing he would say. But she sensed him nowhere on this hill. Perhaps he had finally finished with his work, and no longer needed to oversee this matter.

Then she spotted the shape of a stain on the ground by her master's beam, a faint shadow, thrown by the ugly, overcast sky. The beam's shadow took on a strange shape, a form, the slow curling of a serpent, circling at the base of the post. So the Hollow Man had come at last, no longer needing a human form.

The shadow curled about the thick wooden base of the beam, then uncurled and seemed to slither across the ground. It slithered towards the shadows of an outcropping of rock. And Eden saw the fox once more, sitting still as a stone in a narrow cleft under the outcropping. The fox looked out from the dark hole with feverish eyes. The serpent shadow slithered toward his lair and he twitched his nose in disgust, then shivered.

As the shadow drew closer he bolted like quicksilver out

of the hidey-hole, and vanished into the brush without a look back. He wanted no part of that crawling thing. The serpent shadow slithered on into the hole. Shadows met with shadows, and the serpent disappeared.

The day wore on. The onlookers sat on flat rocks in a rough circle, and others gathered in twos and threes to watch and wait. Those who knew the man, or knew *of him*, sat quietly among themselves. Two others had been sentenced to the hill that day, and those two criminals drew a handful of onlookers—perhaps the men they had robbed, or women they had bedded. It didn't matter, their end would be the same. And lastly, the curious appeared, a few heartless souls desiring a closer look at death.

But they were just a few.

No man sought this ground.

No man chose it of his own free will.

For this fetid hill stank of dried blood, untold bodies and decay.

The Romans had stripped Eden's master of his robe as he dragged the beam up the slope and then pored over his other garments, discarded as he stumbled up the hill. Turban, robe and girdle, they passed the clothes among them so as to soften the flat rocks where they sat for they knew their limbs would soon grow weary. Padding for the endless watch was always welcome.

As the beam was raised Eden saw a long tunic slip from her master's body—but before it touched the soiled ground one Roman soldier pulled his knife from its scabbard and caught it on the blade. With a few shorts stroke he could split the thing among them for extra padding. But the carpenter soldier stayed his fellow's hand. This seamless, finely woven tunic was too precious to cut into patches no matter how hard the rocks under their bones.

Eden saw her master's cracked lips move speaking indistinct words:

Forgive ... forgive them ... forgive everyone

Eden's master must have spoken out loud because the Roman soldiers glanced up at the man on the beam. They shrugged. No soldier begged forgiveness. And for once Eden saw the Roman's true faces, hard and blank like stone. Mercy was something soldiers offered to others but never expected. There was nothing to forgive. Legionaries did their duty. No more, no less. And that's all that mattered.

Now as they sat the long hours, the carpenter soldier fished some dice from his purse and tossed them on the ground. Let some of them at least gamble for these things. One after the other, each Legionary took a throw. Last of all, the carpenter soldier took his turn. And as luck had it, his own dice rolled his way.

His men looked up at him with dark, suspicious eyes.

He won too often for their tastes.

But the carpenter soldier did not covet his prize.

Telling his men, "I'm not keeping it. Sell it later when we're done. Back to his mother if you want, surely one of the women made it for him. For now, it can sit beneath me."

He had brought with him a low wooden stool with his own name carved on it. Years of sitting upon his own mark waiting for men to die had worn away the letters. He carefully folded the tunic, placed it on the stool and sat, covering his name once more.

The soldiers had brought with them drink and food, but did not touch it. They started a smoky fire, burning dirty wood to cover the horrid smell of this ground. And from time to time a Roman stirred the embers of the fire with the tip of his spear to keep it going. They threw a few coins at an old man to fetch armfuls of wood for them from down below. As the day wore on you could hear the old man huffing and puffing each time he brought another sling of sticks and branches to the top of the hill. Down and back, down and back—

Another hour passed. And then another.

The day wore on as the crowd silently watched; the only sound the wind sighing across a broken sky, while the clouds overhead held their breath in anger.

Eden didn't move from the shelter of Maryam's arms. Somehow they seemed to be crouching on the one patch of ground not soiled by an overpowering stench, a tiny patch of ground with a thatch of grass poking up like close-cropped hair. Nearby, under a low bush, three brave mice stood silently watching from the safety of a tangle of thorns, their eyes glued to the men hung on the wood. They whispered nervously among themselves as if they feared they might be next. Eden could not hear what they were saying, but it didn't matter. Their whiskers twitched, their eyes gleamed and they wrung their paws in dismay, too afraid to stay and too afraid to flee.

Flies hovered about her master's mouth and eyes, and Eden heard the woman beside her muttering, attempting to command the flies to depart and trouble their master no more. But the flies didn't listen and Maryam fell silent.

The hours passed.

The men on their wooden beams gasped hopelessly for air. Legs weakened, limbs trembled and their bodies sank. With great effort one of them tried to talk to the other, to speak a few words, but he could barely make a sound, and Eden could not hear them. She felt her master trying to comfort the other men, perhaps to say that this would not endure forever, that something greater was at hand, but she could not make out the words. A cloak of silence seemed to wrap the dog's head. All human tongues were muted in this place, as if the Almighty wanted to keep Eden innocent of darkest human thought.

Her master cried to the sky, begging pity for his pain. Eden heard the cry, but only as a voice tearing at the clouds above. As if to hear him, the sky swirled overhead. And Eden watched, helplessly, those on the beam and those waiting below. The carpenter soldier dipped a ball of sponge into a jar of wine, and then placed it on a stick. The soldier stood on his stool and the wet sponge reached her master's face. The wine ran down his chin and some into his throat. Enough for a few more words.

Did he speak? Was it him?

Or someone else?

Yes, him. Eden heard it.

It is finished …

The world fell silent and the wind took what little of him remained alive.

The merest breath …

A gust, and Eden's master was gone.

For many moments a great stillness hung over the men on their wooden beams and over the people watching. The soldiers looked up from their smoky pit. The fire itself seemed to die. And the deep silence sank into the ground beneath Eden's paws.

The carpenter soldier took a spear from his fellow and went to the wooden beam. He touched it once upon the rib of the hanging man. The flesh did not jump. He pressed it in, and blood and water flowed from the open seam. There was nothing left.

Eden felt a great chasm open inside her. And she realized now that the man she had followed all this time, mile after mile, had faded from her with every step she took. She knew him better when she was a puppy always underfoot in the family's shop. She knew him better as his friend in the wilderness staring at the Hollow Man on the side of the cliff. She knew him better when the rams and goats came to save them, and when she first met the donkey Samson. But since that time he walked from the great water to the great city, since the time he made the strangers well, since the time he saved her from the storm standing by the boat, since all the time of miracles, she did not know him anymore.

He had passed into something greater than that man who loved her. Half shadow, half hope. For he had loved more and more people. And the many places and many creatures of his past clung to him, but only as creatures of the past. And she was one of those. And this emptiness poured through her like grains of sand through open hands until the hands were empty.

Perhaps the Roman soldiers were right, perhaps in a good way.

During their last great journey her master had become all things to all creatures.

Maryam's hands loosened around her neck. The air on this ugly hill swirled overhead, a bitter smoke. Eden felt a queer kind of dizziness that welled from the inside. A great flock of birds flew up from the city below them, circled in a wide arc and kept circling as though the earth itself was no place to land. The sky overhead grew even darker. From every corner of the bald hill the rats began to flee. Eden watched them scamper off, leaping from rock to rock and snaking through every little gully, tails shivering in fear and squealing all at once, running for their lives.

And then the ground beneath their feet began to tremble, shaking the city, the hill, and even tipped the wooden beams with hanging men from side to side.

A rolling thunder came down from heaven and kept roaring until everyone cowered, covering their heads. Cold rain slashed down, cutting as ice, and quickly filled every hole and pockmark. The Roman soldiers clutched their spears and shields, but the shaking earth and roaring air tore the weapons from their hands and the metal clattered to the ground. Then, just as suddenly as it came, the roaring stopped.

And the cold rain passed over the hills toward the horizon.

The carpenter soldier stooped to pick up his spear. The blood from the man's wound still stained the tip despite the rain, and he ran his finger along the edge. He muttered to himself, suddenly ashamed for all he had done and witnessed, and the dog heard his words.

"Righteous blood of a righteous man."

The first bold, clear words Eden understood since she had come to this ugly place.

The carpenter soldier spoke again:

"I saw no evil in him."

Faintly, a forlorn wail rose up from the city and all those standing on the hill turned their faces to look at the high walls. The temple doors stood out like Goliath's gate. The towering curtains draped in the entranceway, now hung in tatters, ripped apart by the wind.

And all the temple worshippers and priests standing in the temple courtyard looked like grains of wheat milling about inside a stone box. They wrung their hands in grief beseeching heaven, tiny, terrified creatures with no place to call home.

No one who stood on the hill could tell if it was sundown or merely dark. But the time had come to relieve the wooden beams of their lifeless burdens. A ladder was brought and winding sheets. And many hands came to return the three men to the earth. The two criminals first. Their crosses, loosed by the rumbles of the earth, toppled easily. Once fallen, they lay on the cold ground unattended, with none to mourn them.

Eden broke from Maryam's arms and went to her master's beam. She could barely reach his feet standing on her hind legs, but her paws scratched the wood. A drop of blood had run down her master's leg and clung stubbornly to his toe.

She whined.

The drop fell to her nose and before she knew what she did, she licked it off.

Plain blood, with that tang of iron and salt and sweat.

The carpenter soldier lent his tools so that they could pry the spikes free without tearing more of the flesh, and before Maryam crossed the dead hands upon his breast, Eden managed to put her head under his fingers, for one last moment, just a moment, as he used to pet her.

One last touch.

But there was no one there.

Everlasting

Fear not, little flock; for it is your Father's good pleasure to give you the kingdom.

For where your treasure is, there will your heart be also.

Luke 12: 32–34

Two Nights and a Day
✷ ✷ ✷

They laid the winding sheet upon the ladder, making a stretcher. But before they could place their master on this makeshift sling the Romans left their fire pit and took the ladder away.

"The ladder is Pilate's," one of them said. "Not the priests'." And the soldiers prepared to lug their ladder down the slope and back to the garrison.

To those clutching the body of Eden's master one of them said, "Carry him arm by arm and leg by leg if you care for him so much."

But not the carpenter soldier. He turned his face away.

The winding sheet became their master's stretcher for the steep descent to the bottom, then to a lower rise and the resting place prepared. Eden followed Maryam silently down the face of the ugly hill. The bearers stumbled as they went, but each time a foot slipped, a knee or elbow met the ground, they righted themselves. On this last trip their burden was not so great, the body lighter than the bundles of sticks the old man had brought for the Romans' fire.

And before the sun set that day, the tomb accepted him and Eden watched the mourners roll a great stone into place.

The salty taste of her master had vanished from her mouth.

As the night drew close Eden's belly twisted in hunger and her tongue swelled, growing thick with thirst. She sat with Maryam under the shoulder of a great boulder. The ground hard, scarcely any grass, but the woman folded their master's cloak and it cushioned them, keeping the cold from seeping into their bones.

Maryam's hand came to Eden's neck and the dog rested her head in the woman's lap. The tomb of their master waited silently in the dark, and they could barely see the outline of the stone covering the entrance.

Why were they waiting here?

What were they waiting for?

Eden did not know.

The moon showed its silver face through a stand of spindly trees on a distant hill and lit the rock tomb. The surface shone whitely, lighting the ground where they sat. Time passed.

Quietly other women joined them, one here, and another there, in twos and threes. Not sitting closely, but scattered across the wide ledge where they could find a touch of shelter, on a rock or beside a boulder. They covered their heads with their shawls to keep warm, which under the moon made them seem part of the earth.

Silent witnesses who watched the stone face of the tomb.

But witnesses to what? Eden could not say.

Suddenly the sound of footfalls on the path rose up from below. Not human feet, for men and women always scraped and shuffled when then moved. But the sound was hard, clear steps. And to her astonishment Eden saw Samson's old gray nose nodding up and down as he climbed. His long ears bobbed with every footfall. He carried a great load of branches on his back, and round his strong neck dangled water skins, sloshing from side to side. While the old man from the horrible hill quietly followed the donkey upward.

And the littlest of the lambs came with him too! Eden watched as the littlest lamb picked her way daintily along the steep path. A tiny bell about her neck jingled brightly through the gloom, the moonlight catching it at every step.

"We thought I'd find you here," Samson told Eden.

"You're burdened now!" the dog exclaimed.

"Yes, but it's an easy burden," Samson told her. "Sticks for this old man. And water for those who wait in the dark. You see, I can bring enough—more than he can carry."

"And look at you, you little rascal," Eden said to the littlest lamb, "someone gave you jewelry!"

"Of course, I keep them company!" exclaimed the littlest lamb. "Marking their coming and going with the sound of my bell!"

"More than that," the gray-faced donkey told Eden. "The bell keeps us from being lost. Like a herald in the night," Samson said, "whether rising from deep ravines or calling over great mountains, no wind can drown out the sound of this bell. A clear voice in the air, a voice of everything to come—"

"And yet its ring is so tiny you barely notice it," said the littlest lamb.

"Like you," Eden said.

"Yes, like me," said the littlest lamb. "Just like me."

The three animals fell silent.

Eden recognized this old man, the same who had brought the Romans firewood on that terrible hill. All this time ignored as one not even worthy of notice, just a few coins tossed in his direction. Yet on this night he brought wood to those who had no coins for him. The women unloaded the sticks from

Samson's back and stacked them in a pile to make a fire. The old man let the women take the wood without complaint, and even helped them stack it. Eden saw Maryam fumble with her purse but the old man simply shook his head, placing his hand upon hers. He wanted no money.

Not this night.

At length, the old man passed the skins around, pouring water into empty cups, or tipping it to waiting hands until every parched throat was quenched. And water itself seemed to fill every belly, sating every tongue, and hunger was no more.

Someone struck a spark from flint and iron, the stack of wood caught and night's chill retreated from the ledge. To Eden it seemed a strange kind of campfire, for though Samson had brought a great load of wood, this fire seemed to need no feeding, burning with light and heat but no ash. And so eventually everyone on the ledge was warmed and heads nodded to their breasts. The last thing Eden saw before her eyes closed was that old man staring at her.

He sat off by himself, curiously aloof, seeking neither the fire nor company. Eden realized that since she had first seen him on the Hill of the Skull he had neither spoken nor been spoken to. Not even the Roman soldiers who merely threw him a handful of coins. Nor did he speak now, but simply stared from his spot by the great stone door. Beside him Samson stood silently, occasionally swishing his tail. And the littlest lamb curled by the old man's feet, the bell round her neck tinkling softly each time she stirred in the dark.

And so night passed into morning.

Dawn of the second day.

Eden opened her eyes and picked her head off Maryam's lap. Samson, the littlest lamb and the old man were nowhere to be seen. But she heard the tiny bell tinkling faintly in the dell down below. After a few moments even that hopeful sound vanished, and a cold wind sighed across the ledge. Maryam huddled into herself, clutching the dog closer. The fire had died, thirst and hunger returned. The women on the ledge stared out of their shawls with hollow eyes. A gray sorrow seemed to cloak them all, and some rose from their chosen rock, stepping a few paces away to weep in private.

But Maryam was not among them. The woman's eyes were dry. She did not weep. Nor had she wept with the others on the Hill of the Skull when their master spoke no more, and they brought him down from the beam. Quietly, she refolded the cloak for herself and the dog to sit on the hard ground. And it struck Eden, two days waiting felt like a long, long time.

The cold wind blew a trifle faster over the ledge, ruffling the women's shawls. They tugged their wraps about their faces, looking from eye to eye, as if the wind itself was trying to tell them a secret. But no one understood, as if the wind spoke secret words in a strange tongue from a foreign lands, far away.

Yet through the wind Eden heard the strangest sound, the murmuring of a voice, faint and indistinct. Not a voice of fear or sadness, but full of great tidings. And underneath the voice, there echoed a beating heart, hope and a second chance.

Eden's ears perked up. The faint sounds came from behind the stone door. Eden went to the rock where her master lay and began to smell keenly around the edge. Several of the women cried out and drove Eden from the sealed entrance to the cave, as if it were a place no dog should touch or even sniff.

Maryam beckoned Eden back to the safety of her arms.

"Never mind them," the woman whispered in Eden's soft ear. "Half of them expect nothing and the other half are too fearful to hope for more."

Eden nuzzled the woman's throat and looked into her eyes. Maryam was neither angry nor afraid. And her eyes suddenly brightened, for the faint sound of the littlest lamb's bell drifted up from the dell.

In a few moments, the bell grew louder. The littlest lamb pranced onto the ledge and Samson plodded solidly up soon after. The old man had returned, bringing more firewood and more water in the same water skins. They sloshed against the donkey's strong neck. After unloading Samson as he had the day before, the old man found his spot near the stone door on the narrow ledge and sat.

A new man followed the first. A younger man, and like the elder one, a silent type and laden down with sacks. He rested the sacks at his feet and joined the old one, sitting on a bit of stony edge that didn't seem wide enough to hold either man. But neither of them stirred, not even to draw their cloaks about them as the wind swept up from the dell tugging shawls across every woman's face. Neither man seeming cold nor tired in any way, just curiously hopeful and expectant.

The heavy scent of baked bread, dried fruits and burnt meat seeped from the sacks, flowing along the ground like fragrant smoke. Everyone knew what the sacks held—*food*—yet no one made a move to paw through them. As if they were not to be plundered yet, not yet. This was not the time to eat.

For her part, Eden had no appetite and she looked at the faces of the women sitting there. No gleam of hunger, just the brick of sadness, the rusty hook of fear. But as for Maryam sheltering Eden in her arms, the woman looked at the dog with cool certainty. Maryam knew something the others did not, and stared hard at the cave, through the very rock. As if the woman could move the stone door with her will alone.

The sun began to set again. How it moved across the heavens so quickly, Eden could not explain. One moment it stood high overhead, then the next it slid toward the horizon, reddening the sky. The wood and kindling Samson had lugged from below were built into a fire. Yet this time for some reason it did not drive away the chill, and the silence of the women grew until it covered the ledge like a heavy weight.

In the dead of night, Eden opened her eyes. That sound again came from behind the door stone. And she could smell that familiar scent.

Her master.

Not musty like the robe on which she and Maryam curled, but strong and vibrant. The scent of life struggled out from under the stone. And from where they sat on the uncomfortable ledge the two silent men, the younger and the old, stared at Eden. Each one seemed to smile, with that same cool certainty the dog had seen in the Maryam's eyes earlier that day.

The faint voice on the wind grew more distinct in Eden's sharp ears, the murmurs behind the stone door grew louder, the scent of her master growing stronger than she ever recalled. Eden couldn't stand it any longer.

She couldn't stand it—

Eden ran to the great door stone and stood on her hind legs.

Paws up, scratching, scratching. *Master, I hear you. Master, I'm here! He's in there, let him out! Let him out!*

Several of the women cried out in anger, rushing from their places to drive Eden away from the forbidden stone, to strike her. But the two strangers, the younger and the older strangers, stared with eyes that seemed to flash … strong, silent eyes. The women froze in place, squatting where they crouched.

Maryam gently took the dog from the face of the stone, bringing Eden back with her to their place on the pad.

"I know," she whispered in the dog's soft ear. "I felt him too. I feel him now."

And Eden realized what Maryam really meant, that these two days' waiting felt like such a long, long time, but this too had passed somehow. And now they stood at the end of a journey and the beginning of a new one.

Eden settled down once more, her head resting in Maryam's lap. The littlest lamb's bell tinkled softly as she curled up by Samson. The donkey stood stoically in the dark, not even swishing his tail. The last thing the dog saw that second night as her eyes fluttered closed was the two men, the younger and old, sitting on the narrow ridge of stone by the flat face of the covered cave. They seemed to shimmer in the dark, as if inner candles lit them, or distant lightning flickered from within. A glow that made her feel safe even as she slept.

And as she slept Eden dreamed. She could see herself nestled in Maryam's arms. Nearby, the two men, the younger and the old, rose from their uncomfortable strip of stone. They went to the face of the tomb and gently rolled the door stone away. And the great stone moved at their slightest touch and the entrance was unsealed.

And as she looked inside, the younger walked into the open grave, while the older stood by the open doorway. Eden tried to peer inside the tomb, through the mouth of the low cave, even tried to rise as she had tried before, to force her way in, but in her dream she couldn't move from Maryam's arms.

The dog could smell the scent of her master, so strong now it filled her head as it never had before. The scent of polished leather and of clean clothes and washed skin, she could smell the scent of fragrant oil and of apricots, of oranges and honey dripping from the comb. Eden could smell the scent of green grass and warm dry straw, of falling water over rocks and pine needles in shady woods like angels' breath in the very air.

The younger man within the tomb knelt where Eden could see him, while the older stood guard at the open hole. Eden felt as though they were about to speak, to say something about what was happening, and finally Eden crawled from the nest of the woman's arms—

And she woke.

Dawn had come again.

Sunlight poured into the open mouth of an empty tomb.

The strange men were gone, and the women rushed to touch the stone door and feel about the edges of the cave's mouth. There were cries of dismay and amazement. The empty tomb moaned quietly as though knowing it would never be filled.

Samson poked his long gray nose at the opening as there was no room for him to enter, but the littlest lamb trotted in and out, then ran right up to Eden and Maryam.

"He's near, I know he's near. Can you feel him? He's almost *here*!"

Eden didn't know what to say. The dog left the comfort of Maryam's arms and went through the cave's mouth. The emptiness yawned at her, and one of the women folded her master's winding cloth, wrapping it tighter and tighter, as if to keep the essence of the man from escaping the shroud.

But the winding cloth meant nothing to Eden, and all the

scent she smelled before had now gone. Vanished. And she stood in a dry, empty cave.

Only the sacks of food remained. Loaves and fishes and meat partly spilled upon the ground, waiting for any to take. And the women broke the bread, passing the food between them.

Maryam rose from the shoulder of the stone where she had sat for two days.

Slowly she approached the cave and knelt to look inside. All who saw the empty cave paid her little mind, until she began to weep quiet tears. But then they paid her mind as she began to speak in a quiet voice. Talking, speaking as it were to the air, as she once had talked to flies. Talking to the empty tomb, "Where have they put him? Do you know? Tell me. If you know, tell me."

But no one answered. And Maryam fell silent once more.

Eden left the cave and went to Samson and the littlest lamb.

"The men you carried wood and water for are gone," she told them. "You belong to no one again. And our master is gone. There is no one here. But as the littlest lamb says, I feel him close too. Let us search for him, at least this day."

Without a word Maryam rose from the empty hole in the side of the rock. She straightened her robe and skirt, silently bid the women farewell with a wave of her hand, then silently walked from the ledge until it broadened to a path. Where Maryam was heading none of the animals knew. But they knew they wanted to follow her, even if she led them nowhere.

Only a few steps up the path they caught the woman and fell in line. And what struck the dog, the donkey and lamb was that all the mice in the fields had appeared again. They stood upon every rocky outcropping, along the stony path, beside every tree. Thousands upon thousands lined either side of the way upon which they tread.

And not only the mice, but the fox himself had reappeared. Explaining as they passed:

"Last night I found a hole to sleep in and woke to find these mice upon my threshold. Perhaps I shall hunger for mice and rats again, but now I hunger for other things. At least for today. At least for now."

At the next turning the crowds of silent mice parted in awe at the sight of the companions—the woman, the dog, the donkey and the lamb—while the fox trotted along, keeping a safe distance but keeping up all the same.

Maryam reached the low wall of a tended garden. Nothing to be planted yet, for it was much too early, yet this was the time to turn the soil and the Gardener stood behind the low wall, planting his wooden spade in the dirt and turning it over. Clod after clod, so it might take spring air and soak up the sun's light.

Maryam paused for a moment to stare at the Gardener; tears sprang to her eyes again and she let them flow. But to Eden the scent of the Gardener told her everything: polished leather, clean clothes and washed skin, of green grass, warm dry straw and the scent of apricots. She smelled the scent of oranges too and nearby a cluster of bees hovered about their comb in the open trunk of an old olive tree. Samson stopped in his tracks with the littlest lamb. While the fox found the shadow of the olive tree to watch and wait and listen.

Eden jumped over the stone wall, stepping in the Gardener's dirt, and ran to greet him. But the Gardener held up a hand and the dog halted a few footfalls away.

"Why do thou weep?" the Gardener asked Maryam, across the stone wall. "Who do thou seek?"

And the woman, wiping the tears from her face with the back of her hand implored the man, "Sir, if you have borne him here, tell me where he lies and I will carry him away."

The sun climbed from the horizon's hill and the animals could see the dew upon the ground. And every mouse in the field was drinking from each drop that lay on rock or a fallen leaf. Eden saw the Gardener smile and she crouched on the soft dirt. The dog knew him now.

And Maryam knew him too, as ever she had. The woman reached out across the wall to touch him once more. Imploring him to come to her, or at least let her come to him. But their master did not go to her or to Eden either. He planted the gardening spade in the earth, letting it stand upright. And the littlest lamb paced back and forth before the low stone wall and under Samson's legs in terrible frustration. For she too wished to go to him. Pacing back and forth and bleating, *come, Samson, jump the wall, you can do that, jump the wall and go to him!*

"I cannot move from here," Samson told the littlest lamb. "Don't ask me why, but I cannot. That garden is not to be trampled. Some day we may enter. But not today."

The littlest lamb still fretted, skipping back and forth.

A sparrow flew in from the old olive tree and landed on the low stone wall. The sparrow hopped up and down in front of the lamb's pink nose and chirped.

"See here now," said the sparrow. "You needn't fret. His eye is on you too."

And with that a sudden calm descended. The mice in the field sighed as one and the fox drowsily blinked his eyes. Eden sniffed the broken dirt and it smelled clean and hopeful. And she knew the time had not yet come to touch her master, for he stood between heaven and earth. That time would come later. Later she would sit by his side, she would play with him and he would pet once more, but not today. Today there was a road ahead.

Eden could see the road now, very clearly winding on ahead. It crossed every threshold and led into every home.

"All right," the littlest lamb sighed at last, and stopped her pacing. "All right, I can wait. I can wait."

Maryam bent to look closer at the top of the garden wall. Amongst the stonework that made the wall, two small stones sat by themselves. A black stone and a white.

Eden sniffed them, just two stones. Ah, you could always tell if they had traveled in a purse or in pocket. You could always tell if they had rubbed together for a long, long time—but these two stones had not. Neither showed their insides; they were fresh and untouched as if born from the earth this very day. Maryam smiled. She picked up the stones and weighed them in her hand. The Gardener smiled and Maryam understood. These were her two stones, her very own. She bid their master farewell. Farewell for now.

The woman left the garden wall and walked on ahead. There was purpose in her stride and no weariness and she knew where she was going. To find the companions, to find every traveler who may have seen the man, but first to the house where the companions were in hiding. They should hide behind closed doors no longer. They had work to do as well.

The animals left the Gardener behind the garden wall and once more trotted to catch up. Maryam was glad to see them and put her arm over Samson's neck as they walked along.

"Where shall we go now?" the donkey asked.

Eden ran on ahead. "Everywhere," she barked.

"Who shall we tell?" asked the littlest lamb.

"Everyone!" Eden said.

About the Author

✳ ✳ ✳

Keith Korman is a literary agent and novelist. Over the years he has represented many nationally-known writers of fiction and non-fiction at his family's literary agency, Raines & Raines. The idea for Eden first came to him as a child when he saw the little calf jump across the stable in the prelude to William Wyler's Ben Hur. And he's been thinking about it ever since.

www.ingramcontent.com/pod-product-compliance
Lightning Source LLC
Chambersburg PA
CBHW060518100426
42743CB00009B/1370